THE COLOUR OF DARKNESS

D0367358

Regards from Scotland

gavin@valuetheperson.com

The Colour of Darkness

A personal story of tragedy
and hope in Rwanda

Lesley Bilinda

Hodder & Stoughton

LONDON SYDNEY AUCKLAND

British Library Cataloguing in Publication Data
A record for this book is available from the British Library.

ISBN 0 340 64279 3

Printed and bound in Great Britain by
Mackays of Chatham PLC, Chatham, Kent

The paper and board used in this paperback are natural
recyclable products made from wood grown in sustainable
forests. The manufacturing processes conform to the
environmental regulations of the country of origin.

Hodder and Stoughton
A division of Hodder Headline
338 Euston Road
London NW1 3BH
www.madaboutbooks.com

In memory of

Charles

and as a tribute
to the million and more Rwandans
who died untimely deaths
during and after the genocide of 1994

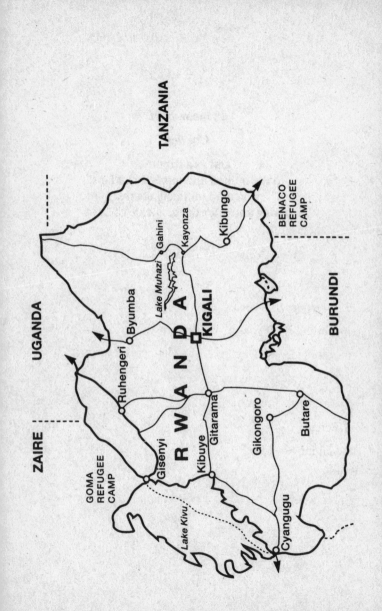

Contents

Acknowledgments   viii

1 Early Days in Rwanda   1

2 Life in Gahini   22

3 Marriage to Charles   44

4 Increasing Tensions and Insecurity   61

5 Killing Beyond Belief – The Genocide Begins   70

6 Agony and Uncertainty in the UK   92

7 Return to Rwanda   114

8 Benaco   140

9 Gahini Revisited   167

10 Isla   183

11 Discovering the Truth in Butare   202

12 Picking Up the Pieces   213

Acknowledgments

I do not know how I would have survived the long, agonising months from April 1994 were it not for the constant love, unending patience and thoughtful support of my sister Sue, together with her husband Cameron and children Tim, Jo, Ben, Sam and Abi. I could never, ever thank her enough. Indeed I would like to thank each member of my family for their love and understanding.

I am also very grateful to Tear Fund, for the quality and sensitivity of their support, and in particular to Sue Mills, Jennifer Loughlin and Peter Chirnside for their exceptional kindness to me, far beyond the call of duty.

The Nzacahayo and Gatwa families in Edinburgh were for me an invaluable link with Rwanda and empathised with me in my heartaches. Thank you.

I have been amazed and deeply humbled by the wide network of Christians throughout the world, so many of whom I do not even know, who have prayed for me, for Charles and for Rwanda. I am extremely grateful and hope this book will demonstrate to them just some of the ways in which God has been answering their prayers.

Thanks are due to many more – but may the glory

go to my Lord and Saviour Jesus Christ, to whose infinite love and undeserved mercy I owe all that I am, and everything that I have.

The experiences of individuals which have been recorded in this book are, to the best of my knowledge, accurate, although I have changed the names of many of the Rwandans in order to protect their identities. However, the passage of time and frequent telling of events (as well as my imperfect memory!) may mean that some details are inaccurate, and for that I apologise.

It must also be said that it is often extremely difficult to determine the truth, as different people may have vastly differing interpretations of the same situation. I have tried therefore not to make judgments, but simply to relate events as I perceived them or as they were reported to me.

1

Early Days in Rwanda

'At least there isn't a smell of dead bodies any more.' I was speaking half to myself and half to Jennifer, sitting on a grassy slope overlooking the Rwandan capital of Kigali.

It was October 1994 and I had returned to Rwanda, the breathtakingly beautiful Central African country that had been my home for the previous five years. This was my first opportunity to come back after the civil war that had taken place within the country from April to June 1994. My present visit was only for a month, but it was going to be a very tough month. I was fully aware of that, as was Tear Fund, the Christian relief and development agency for whom I had been working.

Not wanting me to have to face the pain of returning alone, I agreed with Tear Fund that it would be better for me to be accompanied to Rwanda. Jennifer Loughlin was Director of Personnel for the organisation, and had also become a friend over the years I had been with Tear Fund. I was very glad that Jennifer and I would be together for the first two weeks of my visit.

We sat quietly on the grass as I adjusted to being back, and allowed Africa once again to seep slowly

through my whole being. The smells were so familiar –
the strong sweet magnolia mingling with a faint stench
of rubbish, and the smoke of a thousand cooking fires
lingering in the air. Here, on our first day back in
Rwanda, it was a smell of the Africa I remembered.
The acrid sharpness of rotting human flesh was not to
hit us until later.

The distant sound of traffic was almost drowned by
flies buzzing around, children's voices laughing and
playing nearby, and the rich variety of song from the
tropical birds. The setting was deceptively peaceful.
We were sitting in the garden of what had been, before
the war, the home of missionary friends of mine. A
large green expanse on several layers, it was divided
up by avocado trees and beds of brilliantly coloured
flowers, and had a wonderful view down over the city
and to the hills beyond.

The warm sun and gentle breeze on my face caused
my mind to wander in several directions all at once. If
I shut my eyes I could see myself trekking up and
down the hills with Anatolie, my former Rwandan
colleague in the community health programme, and
one or other of our health workers. It was so vivid – as
if it were yesterday, as if we would go back to Gahini,
the village where we lived, after a weekend break away
and carry on where we left off. But I knew we never
would. Anatolie was dead. I shook my head in disbelief; it seemed impossible. Surely when I go back to
Gahini she will be there, just as she always was. It
suddenly seemed as if time had stood still for the last
six months.

Six months? Was it really six months since I was last
here? Yes, I guess it was. It was now the beginning of
October and I had left Rwanda at the end of March.

How different it was this time, coming back to the country that had become my adopted homeland, a country I had grown to love so much.

I flicked a few persistent ants off my skirt, and decided to move out of the powerful rays of the sun. Checking that there were no rotting avocados hiding in the coarse grass, I settled myself down in the shade of a tree. It seemed like no time at all since I had first stepped off the plane in Kigali, back in 1989, naïve and excited, and blissfully oblivious as to what lay ahead.

It was the smells that hit me then, too, as I took my first steps out of the plane into the heavy African heat. I paused for a few seconds, full of anticipation, as the passengers in front of me negotiated the narrow steep steps down on to the tarmac. Taking a long, deep breath I filled my lungs with the warm, smoky air. 'Mmm. This is *Africa*.'

We struggled across the tarmac in a scraggy line, each one loaded with umpteen bags and cases. Inside the airport terminal I joined the queue that had formed, and waited to present my passport, visa and yellow fever certificate. I was so excited that my hand was almost shaking too much to be able to fill in the debarkation form.

I looked over the barrier, and down into the waiting hall on the ground floor. To my relief, I spotted Rob, a British doctor from Gahini Hospital, who was waving madly at me. He was standing with two Rwandans, a little apart from everyone else. I dumped my bags down and waved back enthusiastically, then rejoined the slow-moving queue.

Having hauled the rest of my luggage off the carousel, I followed the lead of the seasoned travellers and dragged it across to one of the customs men. He poked and prodded through my clothes and books.

'Are you French?' he asked me in French. A look of confusion came over his face when I told him I was Scottish.

'Do they speak French there then? You sound French.'

At that time, most people in Scotland had never heard of Rwanda, so it was hardly surprising that Rwandans should not know about Scotland. He was pleased to discover that we speak English in Scotland!

'Give me something to read in English!' he continued, not even glancing up from my belongings. I was rather taken aback by his forwardness. What a cheek! But he was laughing, so I was not sure if he was being serious. He was looking at some books in my case, but I was not prepared to part with them having only just arrived. Half-heartedly, I offered him a midwifery journal I had been reading on the plane – it seemed to make him happy enough! The customs check was over.

It was great to see Rob again. I had got to know him and his wife Trisha, a physiotherapist, during a previous visit to Rwanda (a short voluntary placement at Gahini Hospital back in 1987), and I was looking forward to being with them again. He introduced me to the Rwandans who were standing with him.

'This is the couple you'll be staying with for the first few weeks – Etienne and his wife Emeralde.' We shook hands, greeting each other politely in French. 'I thought it would be good if they could come and meet you today,' Rob said.

Etienne and Emeralde smiled at me. 'We are happy to meet you. Welcome to our country.' I took an instant liking to them, with their round, smiling faces, and was relieved to hear that Etienne could speak a little English.

'Thank you,' I responded. 'I'm very pleased to be here.'

Back in Scotland at the end of October 1989 it was turning quite cold, but here the weather was glorious. The rains had begun that month, so as we headed out of town on the road back to Gahini, I was struck by how green and luscious everything looked.

It took about one hour and fifteen minutes from the airport in Kigali to Gahini by car, and at least two hours in a taxi, I was told, when I asked how far it was. Kilometres or miles mean nothing to someone who walks everywhere or travels by public transport, as most Rwandans do. I was just thinking about black taxi cabs at home, and wondering why they should take so much longer, when suddenly our car swerved into the middle of the road.

'That was *close!*' Rob exclaimed. 'These taxi drivers *never* look!'

I turned round to look at the 'taxi' to which Rob was referring – a far cry indeed from the British black cab. Speeding along close behind us was the most clapped-out old minibus I had ever seen. It was amazing that the driver could see anything at all through the badly cracked windscreen! The minibus was crammed full of people, and piled high above and behind with a motley collection of dirty yellow jerrycans, a mattress, a couple of holdall bags, and several bulging sacks. What a sight!

But there was so much else to look at. Life, movement, colour, activity in every direction. The road was lined with people – women wrapped in a variety of brightly coloured cloths, sometimes a baby's head just visible on their backs, and a large basin or sack of produce balanced on their heads; men on black bicycles, their cargo four or five well-filled jerrycans securely strapped on, or perhaps another brightly clad woman and baby, sitting side saddle on the back. It all looked extremely precarious to me!

Blue-dressed girls and khaki-clad boys ran and laughed in groups at the side of the road, often straying into the middle. Even a toot from the horn did not seem to dampen their enthusiasm for playing in the path of oncoming vehicles. Apart from the danger of the unpredictable taxi drivers there did not seem to be a strong chance of an accident with another vehicle – we met very few. Much more likely, I thought, would be an accident with one of these lively children. Or perhaps with one of the scraggy brown cows with enormous wide horns, wandering off from the group. The frantic whacks, from the stick of the little boy looking after them, apparently had little impact on these independent beasts. All in all, driving on these roads seemed to me to be quite a dangerous occupation!

The road twisted and wound round between the hills. There were no towns to speak of, just individual houses – everywhere! All along the roadside, down in the valleys, and up the slopes of the hills behind. Most were solid-looking cement-built buildings with tin roofs, but a few were the more traditional round, mud houses with thatched roofs. Almost all had a tall hedge around them, encircling not only the main house, but also one or two smaller mud huts.

The hillside between the houses looked very fertile; large patches of green banana palms were interspersed with ploughed fields. I could see several people digging in the fields, and by their brightly coloured clothes I guessed they were mostly women.

We drove on, chatting together in English mixed with French and what I presumed was Kinyarwandan (the two official languages of Rwanda), although the Kinyarwandan sounded like nothing on earth to me. I wondered how I would ever be able to make out any of the words, let alone speak it. But I was looking forward to the challenge, and was sure that staying with a family would be the best way to go about it.

We were now approaching a small roundabout in the centre of a village. At the side of the road was a signpost marked 'Kayonza'. There were two garages with petrol pumps and several young lads standing around, and a few more houses clustered together. I glanced inside the open doors as we passed and could see shelves filled with goods. Through other open doors I could see groups of men sitting around. These apparently were the shops and pubs. Behind the roundabout were two more signposts; to the right Tanzania, and to the left Uganda. We took the road to the left.

'How far is it to Uganda?' I asked.

'From here it's over a hundred kilometres,' Rob replied. 'The road goes right through the Park, so sometimes you can see some animals. We're nearly home now, though, it's only about 10 kilometres from here to Gahini.'

We rounded another bend and the lake came into view. I remembered it well from my previous visit nearly three years ago, a long, thin, twisty expanse of water stretching almost all the way to Kigali, with finger-like projections down each side. We used to swim there most days, in its murky brown waters. It was a magnificent sight.

My excitement mounted still further as we turned off the smooth tarmac and up a steep rough muddy road. Rob knew it well and expertly avoided the worst of the ruts and pot-holes. Even so, I had to cling on tightly to the dashboard as we were thrown around violently.

I wanted to look everywhere at once. What did I recognise? What had changed? Would I know anyone? 'Stop! Stop! That's Louis isn't it?' I shouted. I had caught sight of a tall, slim man walking by the side of the road. He looked just like the chap I had got to know a little last time, and had sporadically kept in touch with since.

Rob stopped the car and I jumped out. 'Louis!' There was a moment of hesitation before his face broke into a huge grin and we threw our arms round each other.

'Lesley! I almost didn't recognise you. You've had all your hair cut off! It's great to see you again.'

Not wanting to hold everyone up, I suggested he meet us up at Rob's and Trisha's house, and then got back into the car.

At Rob's and Trisha's house the tea was ready and waiting for us on the table, in the most enormous thermos flask I had ever seen; but as visitors began to drop in one after another, I realised how essential it was. While the others chatted, I nipped out of the sitting-room door on to the balcony. I stood silently, mesmerised by the spectacular view down over the lake. It felt *so* good to be back, I could hardly believe it was real. A tear began to roll down my cheek. 'Thank you, Lord,' I whispered. 'Thank you for bringing me here.'

Suddenly I felt an arm slip around my shoulders. It

was Trisha. 'Are you OK?' she asked, her voice full of concern.

'Oh Trisha, I'm just *so* happy to be here,' I blurted out, giving her a hug.

'Is *that* what it is,' she laughed. 'Oh well, that's OK then!'

Soon it would be getting dark, so we had to move on. I felt very excited at the thought of seeing my new home for the first time. The rough road took us round the back of the church and hospital, between a cluster of houses and then out into the countryside. It was not far from Gahini, but we had to go very slowly as the car slipped and slithered along the muddy road. In some places the land had been cultivated right on to the track, narrowing it so much that I thought we would be unable to pass. Eventually, carefully avoiding a few banana trees, we drew up outside Etienne's and Emeralde's house.

'Look, isn't that lovely,' Trisha exclaimed. 'They've put up the banana trees to welcome you!'

I looked around to see what she was referring to. It was all so strange to me that I could not tell what was normally there, and what had been done in my honour! Did pink and orange Bougainvillea not normally grow out of banana trees on either side of the gate?

The house seemed to be full of people. Do they all live here, I wondered. My luggage was unloaded by dozens of willing hands and whisked away out of my sight. Everyone was shaking hands with everyone else, even down to the smallest child. I was relieved to be sat down in a chair and just to watch and listen quietly to all the activity going on around me. They all kept looking at me, smiling, and joking with each other. But

I hadn't a clue what they were saying, so I sipped my mug of hot, weak, very sweet tea, and smiled back politely.

The next day I woke up to the sun shining brightly through the small window of my bedroom. I was surprised at how quiet it was outside – surely they were not still in bed? Slowly I ventured out of my bedroom into the sitting-room, and on through to the back of the house.

'Rezire, mwaramutseho!'

I realised Emeralde must be speaking to me, but what was she saying?

'Mwa – ra – mu – tse – ho!' She repeated the same word (or was it words?) to me very slowly. My attempts to say the same back to her brought gales of laughter from the children and the three ladies sitting on the wall at the edge of the house. Oh dear, I thought. This is *not* going to be easy!

With a mixture of sign language, lots of laughter and a babble I could make neither head nor tail of, Emeralde led me back into the house, and showed me a large plastic basin and small jerrycan on the ground just outside my bedroom door. There was warm water in the jerrycan, and a new bar of soap and a clean towel. How lovely! I thanked her as best I could and, putting everything into the basin, together with the toilet roll that had been left for me in my room, I followed her to the back door.

But there was a problem: mud! The 'toilet' and 'shower' were beyond the cow shed, and between us was a sea of mud. I only had on a pair of flimsy sandals, and my boots were in my tea chest – still somewhere between London and Kigali! But Emeralde had thought of that one too – a pair of spotlessly clean wellington boots were waiting for me at the back door.

I squeezed my size seven feet into the size five boots and hobbled outside. It felt as if all eyes were on me as I squelched my way precariously through the sticky mud, round the side of the empty cow shed, and pushed open the rickety door of the 'shower room'.

The toilet and shower room were pretty much the same. Each was a small shed, about 4 feet square, made of a stick frame, filled up with mud (although with rather too many cracks for my liking!) and with a corrugated tin roof. The difference was that the toilet had a very deep hole in the middle of the packed-mud floor – the 'long drop'.

In time I became accustomed to this rather public routine in the mornings, but the real test came at night-times, when occasionally an excess of beans would cause me to wake up with violent stomach cramps. It was then a race against time to find my torch, throw a *kanga* (a piece of coloured cloth) around my waist, wrestle with the too-small boots and the bolt on the back door (quietly, so as not to wake everyone up), and slip and slide my way over the bumps and through the puddles round to the 'long drop'!

The day after my arrival it was Saturday, and the law obliged all Rwandan citizens to take part in community service on Saturday mornings; however, as I had just arrived, I was exempt. That gave me a chance to explore my surroundings.

Etienne's and Emeralde's house was well built, a solid mud structure with grey-cement on the outside walls and whitewashed inside. Each room had a small glass window with a metal frame. In my bedroom was a heavy wooden bed with a bright hand-embroidered bedspread, a low wooden table, and a rush mat on the packed mud floor. Matching embroidered cloths decorated the window ledge, the table, and even my suitcases.

The uneven white walls had a number of shallow holes – unfortunately just big enough for a cricket to hide in at night. So one of my first priorities was to get hold of an insect spray, for their deafening and rhythmical scratching right by my ears woke me up without fail in the middle of the night. Even with ear plugs, I quickly discovered there was no way I could go back to sleep until I had located the beasts, and then silenced them with a quick blast of insecticide!

The kitchen was outside – another mud construction, somewhat larger than the 'shower'. Stepping inside I could hardly breathe as smoke billowed up from the fires. But as my eyes grew accustomed to the sting of the blanket of smoke, I could make out three cooking pots, each carefully balanced on a triangle of three stones.

'Is this what we are having for lunch?' I tried to ask Emeralde in a mixture of words and actions, indicating the green leaves in the pot. It was clear I had got it wrong when Emeralde and the young girl stoking the fire both burst into guffaws of laughter. No, these were banana leaves used as a lid, carefully tucked over the food simmering underneath. I laughed as well, realising how ludicrous I must sound to them!

Lunch was beans and rice – in fact, we had beans almost every day, sometimes even twice a day. Fortunately, I had been a vegetarian on and off for a number of years, so I was already quite fond of beans – but not in the quantity the Rwandans managed to pack away! The first time we had meat, I thought it would be a great treat, but it did not turn out quite how I expected. That night I wrote home to my parents: 'Today we had chicken for lunch (I suspected that when I heard the frantic squawking early this morning!) – the first meat since I've been here. I picked a wing, thinking I could manage that – and found only a couple of mouthfuls of the toughest old boot I've ever chewed! So they gave me the gizzard, which I gnawed my way through politely, and filled up on rice instead.'

Life was never dull in my new home, and there was a constant coming and going of visitors from morning till night. The huge pots of beans could always be stretched to accommodate a few extra, especially the poorer folk in the area who knew they would be welcomed at any time.

Often in the evenings we would congregate in the sitting-room around a single paraffin lamp, and chat for hours on end. Not that *I* did much chatting! I was usually so tired by then, and had no energy left even to attempt to make any sense of what I was hearing. I was always thoughtfully introduced to the visitors by name, but their names all sounded strange to me, and I could not make out who was who among the dark faces in the dimly lit room.

'Don't you remember who this is?' Emeralde would frequently ask me when we met someone on the way to work. 'She came to our house last Wednesday evening.' How on earth she expected me to differentiate between them all, let alone remember their names, I will never know! I later discovered that most Rwandans seem to have an amazing memory, but it took me a long time before I was able to recall more than a few people's names.

Often they took me to visit their friends and umpteen

relatives. Emeralde's elderly but sprightly mother lived in a small house only ten minutes' walk away, together with her three daughters, son and nine grandchildren. The 'old lady', as they called her, reminded me in some ways of my own late grandmother and I really enjoyed these visits to 'Granny's' house. On other occasions it was not unusual for us to spend up to an hour walking to the friends' home, and then sit for ages, not necessarily saying very much. I wrote in another letter home, 'Time has slowed down to first gear ... There's never any hurry and we're invariably late for things. But no one minds!'

I was slowly realising how people mattered so much more than punctuality in Rwanda. One evening a visitor arrived just as we were preparing to go out. Yet no mention was made of our previous plans. Instead, out came the kettle of hot, milky, sweet tea, and the guest was made welcome until such time as she decided to leave. The result was that when we eventually arrived at our hosts' home, the dinner had long since got cold, despite their attempts to keep it warm by wrapping up the dishes in blankets! But sure enough, no one minded.

I was so grateful, though, to have my own bedroom. It meant I could escape to be on my own for a while, and write some letters by torchlight. Being such sociable people, it was probably hard for them to understand why I should choose to be alone.

Sometimes the children's curiosity would get the better of them. 'What does she do in there on her own?' 'She's writing again,' someone would reply. Above the tropical evening chorus of crickets and frogs, I used to hear quiet whispering just outside my door. Looking up in the half dark, I would barely be able to make out three little faces peeping round the door, watching me intently.

The children were tremendous fun to have around. There seemed to be so many of them, but eventually I worked out that there were only five in our family (four boys and one girl, ranging in age from fifteen to five) and the rest were neighbours. Usually they got up very early in the morning to do many jobs around the home before going to school. There was water to be collected in jerrycans from the lake – a good fifteen minutes' walk away; firewood to be searched for, and the fire to be kept going for heating water and making the morning porridge; and the cows had to be taken out on to the nearby hills to graze.

But in the evenings, after it got dark at half-past six, most of the jobs were finished and there was time to relax. Sometimes the children tried to teach me some new words by drawing a picture with chalk on their school slate, and writing the word beside it in Kinyarwandan. 'Inka' – the long horns showed me that was a cow. 'Isitimu' – looked like a torch. 'Umuneke' – banana. 'Rezire' – they pointed at me. I did not understand. They had drawn a stick figure. Did it mean 'person'? I read the word aloud several times, slowly at first, and then more quickly. At last it dawned.

'Rezire – that's me, Lesley! Of course!' I had forgotten how they often mix up their 'l's and their 'r's. Thus Lionel, the other English doctor, became 'Riyoneri', and Lorraine, the Australian physiotherapist, became 'Roreni'. Now it was my turn to laugh!

Learning a language can be hilarious at times, but it can also be unbelievably frustrating. Although Etienne spoke some English, and Emeralde spoke some French, the idea was that they would speak only

Kinyarwandan to me. In this way I would be hearing it all the time, so that my ear would eventually become attuned. And I was to learn to speak by imitating what I heard – a bit like the way a child first learns to speak. 'Great in theory,' I wrote home, 'but in practice it means spending literally hours on end just sitting listening to people talking, picking up perhaps one word every five minutes if I'm lucky; it means having to struggle even to understand and respond to the simplest of questions; not understanding what folk are laughing at, and feeling really out of things, although *longing* to chat with and get to know these folk.'

One Saturday, when I was feeling particularly dis- couraged by my progress in Kinyarwandan, God used a simple picture to encourage me to persevere. We had come to Gahini as usual for seven o' clock in the morning. I wanted to speak to Lionel before starting work, but there was no sign of life at the house that Lionel lived in with his wife Mary and daughter Hannah. So I sat down to wait in the sun on the balcony steps outside. The view before me was strikingly differ- ent from usual. Where normally I had looked down the valley to Lake Muhazi and to the rolling hills stretching far beyond, now it was all totally invisible, shrouded in the morning mist.

As I sat watching, one or two hill tops began to appear in the distance. Then the mist started slipping slowly away in the foreground, revealing trees dotted here and there, and a little bit more of the hills. But still most of the picture was covered in dense greyness. Slowly and steadily more and more of the scene became visible, the valleys between the hills, the fields and houses between the trees, until only the far part of the lake and hills remained covered.

It suddenly struck me how similar this scene was to the process of learning a language. To begin with, the sounds all blended together like a total haze, and I could pick out only a very few disjointed words here and there. Then, as time went by, the words began gradually to connect to each other, but there were still great chunks that remained incomprehensible. I realised then that eventually the details would fall into place, and the overall scene would make sense, even if it took a long long time for the 'distant hills' to come into the picture.

The mist disappearing was a long slow process, happening almost imperceptibly. I would look down for a few moments to watch the ants scurrying about on the path, and when I looked up, there was yet another slope of a hill visible.

Yes, chunks of Kinyarwandan were actually sinking in somewhere in the recesses of my brain, even if I was not always aware of the progress I was making. I had to accept that I could not hurry the process, any more than I could blow away the early morning mist! I would just have to be patient and persevere.

Not all my time was spent with the family. Coming in to the hospital every day for work meant meeting up with other expatriates, usually over morning coffee, sometimes for lunch. They were always interested to hear how I was getting on in my Rwandan home. I was the guinea-pig – no new overseas worker in our area had ever gone to live with a Rwandan family.

I discovered later that a few Rwandans looked on the venture with suspicion – some said 'Etienne and Emeralde are only out to gain favours with the *Bazungu*' (as they called us white people). Yet most had a healthy curiosity – 'Does she eat beans?' 'How does she wash without running water?' 'What do you talk about?' – and my British colleagues displayed a mixture of excitement and concern.

Etienne and Emeralde both had jobs, but their salaries were only enough to cover such things as the children's education, clothes and house maintenance. Luxuries were out of the question, and yet out of their meagre resources, no expense or effort was spared to make me feel welcome and at home.

The contrast between the two lifestyles – my Rwandan family and the expatriate community – was a constant struggle for me. A day off with my Rwandan family would be spent walking over the hills to visit friends, possibly not returning for lunch till mid-afternoon, but a day off with the British crowd was often spent driving for forty-five minutes to Gabiro Hotel in the wildlife park, then lazing by the pool sipping beer and eating pizza and chips!

Holidays for the expatriates often meant a safari in Kenya, or a week on the Mombasa coast, but my Rwandan family always took their holidays in the early rainy season so they could spend each day working the land, preparing it for planting. Even a trip into the capital, Kigali, would be a rare treat for them.

Sometimes I wondered where I fitted in. Should I take a break from time to time, and merge into the social life of the expatriate community? Or should I persevere, trying to identify completely with my hosts, and to leave aside, at least for a while, my own cultural background? It was a difficult dilemma for me.

Part of my reason for requesting to stay with a Rwandan family had been to try to enter as fully as possible into life in the local culture. My work in community health would be impossible without an understanding of their way of life and thinking. I wanted so much to build deep relationships with people, but I knew that that would not be easy as our lifestyles were already poles apart. It seemed to me that spending money on travelling, fancy foods and other luxuries would only serve to deepen the divide between us. And as Christians, I questioned whether we should be using our wealth to help those around us in need, rather than spending selfishly on ourselves.

I grappled with these questions and tried very hard to live simply, but I often became tired and unhelpfully critical of those around me with their relatively affluent lifestyles. It took a long time before I realised that I had failed to take into account my own background.

The dilemmas I was facing were not an issue for the people with whom I lived. They had been brought up in a country where the basic struggle for survival took precedence over everything else; they knew nothing different. But the first thirty years of my life had not been spent in Rwanda. I had been brought up in a culture where leisure, amusement and variety were integral to life, and after a while I began to miss it. I had nowhere near the same endurance, patience and stamina of these amazing people. So I grew to admire them greatly, and reluctantly accepted my need for a bit of Western-style relaxation from time to time.

From a distance the lake looked deliciously inviting, especially after a long day of trekking on muddy roads in the hot sun. My family did not swim – the children were too busy with jobs (although they often had fun messing around in the little lake where they drew water). And it would be unthinkable for a married woman to reveal her thighs by donning a swimming costume! But there was never any shortage of expatriates heading down for a refreshing dip after work – nor was there a shortage of fascinated young children, eager to watch the *Bazungu* larking around in the water.

The grassy clearing edging the section of the lake in which we swam provided a convenient place for a variety of water activities. There were children collecting water for home in all manner of patched-up jerrycans and saucepans. Some had brought a few scrawny cows down to drink from the lake, and we respectfully avoided their viciously long horns. One or two women scrubbed vigorously at the clothes in their soap-filled basins. And I, to my shame (having not yet mastered the art of washing thoroughly in two inches of water in a basin), added to this pollution of the water by making good use of the bar of soap and bottle of shampoo I had brought with me!

Fortunately, some enterprising missionaries had built a solid wooden pier, jutting out into the water, which avoided the necessity of squelching through the leech-infested mud at the edge of the lake. Standing on the end of the pier looking down at the murky brown water, it was impossible to see more than about two or three inches below the surface. Who could tell what other nasty beasties might be lurking in there? It took a lot of courage to dive in! Occasionally a burst of excited yells from the shore alerted us to some danger – perhaps a water snake swimming by. Fortunately, the hippopotamuses, although frequently audible in the rushes at the other side of the lake, very rarely made an appearance on our side.

Despite all these hazards, it really was an idyllic place to swim. The setting sun between five-thirty and six o'clock painted breathtakingly beautiful reds, golds and oranges over the lake. Nothing could be heard except the noisy evening chorus of frogs and insects, and the gentle lap of water on the shore. It was the perfect way to relax at the end of a day.

But now, in October 1994, it was not like that any more. As I sat in the shade at Kigali, I shuddered as I thought about it. The lake had become a mass grave. Hundreds, perhaps thousands, of people from the area had been chopped to death by machete and tossed into it. I had seen pictures of it on the television, but it had all seemed so unreal. Now, though, I was going to have to face it for myself.

Etienne, Emeralde and their children had become refugees, struggling even more now for survival in a vast, sprawling camp in Tanzania. Those who had formed the community of Gahini, which had been my home for nearly five years, were either dead or scattered far and wide. Life would never be the same again.

What would Gahini be like now, I wondered, six months after the massacres began? Would there be anyone I knew still there? Would I be welcome?

We had arranged a lift there for the next day. It was difficult to sleep that night as I thought of what was to come, and my mind buzzed with such mixed emotions: eager anticipation of returning to my home; profound grief at the loss of many friends, and loss of a whole era of life; and the tension of uncertainty, not knowing what I would find when I got there.

But, above all, I wondered whether I might just find some clue as to what had happened to my husband Charles.

2

Life in Gahini

Gahini could not really be described as a town, although it did boast two secondary schools and a primary school, a large Anglican church and a Bible college, and a rehabilitation centre for handicapped people as well as a busy one-hundred bed hospital. It was more of a small community on a hill. Most of the people who had lived in the clusters of houses scattered around the hill had been employed locally, or provided back-up amenities. It had been the sort of place where everyone knew everyone else's business, and most people seemed to be related to each other in some way. Despite its seemingly insignificant size, it was known throughout the world as one of the very first places where the 1930s East Africa Revival began.

The small expatriate group, of which I was immediately a part when I arrived in 1989, was like a community within a community. We were all involved in hospital work of some sort. The two doctors, Rob and Lionel, both had physiotherapist wives, Trisha and Mary. There were also two other full-time physiotherapists, Liz and Lorraine, with a third, Janie, arriving shortly after me. I felt a little outnumbered! Not only was I not a physiotherapist, but I was the only one whose work was not really in the hospital – or so I had thought.

I had originally been accepted by Tear Fund to work alongside another British nurse, Jill, who had lived in Burundi and Rwanda for many years. She was one of those amazing people who can juggle half a dozen different jobs at the same time – manage the community health programme, run the school of nursing, be hospital matron, and organise the pharmacy among other things! But in the end it was too much work for her, so I was assigned the community work in order to allow her time for her other responsibilities. Sadly, some months before I arrived, she had a very serious car accident and had to return home for good.

To my dismay, I arrived in 1989 to find that I was expected not only to develop the community health programme, but also to run the school of nursing – a far cry from the 'some training of nurse aids' that had appeared as item four on my job description! It was some years since I had practised as a staff nurse, and I certainly had no tutoring experience. I did not even *like* hospital work – that was why I had opted for a community job! But it was a very small nursing school, and the six girls currently halfway through their training had already had umpteen setbacks, so were desperate to carry on. Anyway, there was quite simply no one else available to do the job.

It was not at all easy for me, though. There were virtually no textbooks to help me in my lesson preparation, and the cupboard in which Jill had kept the course notes was very firmly locked. The key was nowhere to be found, so eventually I had to break the door. 'Microbiologie. Parasitologie. Laboratoire . . .' How could I possibly teach these subjects? I hadn't a clue! I looked farther along the shelf – 'Hygiene, Premiers Soins . . .' Perhaps I would be able to manage those a little better. But I still had to spend hours each day ploughing through all the notes, and quizzing Rob and Lionel on medical aspects I could not understand.

For two hours every day I would work on the wards with each one of the students in turn. I'm not sure who dreaded these sessions the most – me, or the student, or the nurses in charge of the ward, who all seemed to regard my presence as an unnecessary intrusion. All, that was, except one particular charge nurse, who grovelled every time I appeared: 'Oh Sister, we are so pleased that you have come. We so need a Sister to organise the wards here.' The fact that he had the most disorganised, untidy and dirty ward of the hospital seemed as irrelevant to him as my protestations that I was *not* the Sister, and that it was his job, not mine, to organise his ward!

I quickly found the girls had learned the theory excellently and could repeat their notes verbatim in any test I gave them. But when it came to putting the theory into practice it was a different story.

'*How* do you prevent pressure sores?' I asked for the umpteenth time, as I watched one student vigorously rubbing an elderly gentleman's bony sacrum after giving him a bed bath.

'By making sure his sheets are clean, don't have crumbs or wrinkles, and by turning him regularly,' came the dutiful reply, also for the umpteenth time.

I took a deep breath and picked up a grubby sheet of paper hanging on the end of the patient's bed.

'So why is it that nothing has been marked on his turning chart for the last two days, and the sheet we have just taken off this bed was absolutely filthy?'

It was always a temptation to come down heavily on the poor girls, but I also had to understand the conditions in which they worked. A basic activity such as carrying out a bed bath, which would be considered simple in an average NHS ward back in the UK, was a major task here.

Water first had to be collected (from the lake if the hospital water pump had broken down) and then heated over an open fire. The nurse would be lucky to find a clean sheet, as linen was always in short supply, and the linen cupboard kept locked. We often used to joke that we could have left the most addictive drug sitting in the middle of the floor and no one would touch it, but leave a sheet there, and it would be gone in minutes! Yes, I had to admit that the conditions under which they worked were vastly different from those in St Mary's, Paddington, where I had done my training. But did that mean standards of care should be any less high? It was an issue with which I constantly wrestled.

As well as the training of the student nurses, there were two other areas of work in which I had responsibilities in those early months: involvement in the community health programme, and working in the maternity department.

A night shift in maternity, which I did once a week, ran from five o' clock in the evening to seven-thirty the next morning. It was a long night, but if there were no women in labour, or problems on the ward, then the midwife on call went to bed.

There was a little side room off the main ward with two extremely uncomfortable beds, one for the midwife and the other for the auxiliary assisting. Yet even on a quiet night, sleep was rare. The tiny mosquitoes always seemed to head straight for my ear with their high pitched 'zzzzzz' sound, and I quickly discovered that hunting for them by torchlight or paraffin lamp was a total waste of time.

And it was not just the mosquitoes that kept me awake. One of the auxiliaries was a young mother with a baby. Whenever the baby was ill, she had to be brought to work, together with an older girl to help look after her. A crying coughing baby, together with two whispering, fidgeting adults in a bed only 3 feet away from mine, was definitely not conducive to sleep. However, the worst bit was waking up one night to a scratching and rustling near my ear, and grabbing my torch just in time to see a rat scuttle away under the bed.

I soon discovered that the women's obstetric histories were horrendous. There were few who had not had a stillbirth or a baby die within the first few weeks of life. Some had lost several children, and often did not know the cause. The antenatal consultation cards, with space for details of twelve previous pregnancies, were often not big enough to record all the information.

One evening a woman arrived with a very sick nine-day-old baby. After three stillbirths in the past, she had at last given birth to a live child at home. But her son had become seriously ill with respiratory problems, so she had brought him to hospital. The doctor was called and we stayed up most of the night with that precious baby and its mother. But it was too late; he died in the early hours of the morning. That was my first experience of tragedy in Rwanda. The mother showed no outward emotion as my colleague prayed with her, but a tear rolled silently down my cheek. In the morning she gathered up her few belongings, placed the tiny baby in a cardboard box, and began the long journey home.

Such tragedies, though, were not restricted to the uneducated, poor people of the countryside. Anatolie, my Rwandan colleague in the community health programme, was a well-qualified experienced social worker. Her husband was a teacher in the local secondary school, and they had a lovely little girl of three called Mireille. Anatolie was well through her third pregnancy when I arrived, her second child having died when it was only three days old.

In January 1990, to her absolute delight, Anatolie gave birth to twins. However, within twenty-four hours both babies had developed severe jaundice. The only really effective treatment would have been to give a blood transfusion, but there was nowhere in the country where that was possible for babies. Sadly, although one of the babies, Liliose, did recover fully, the other was very weak and died quite quickly. Anatolie faced her suffering with remarkable patience and courage, but I could not help thinking of how much more could have been done for her had she been living in the West.

Apart from the student nurse training and the weekly night shift in maternity, the bulk of my work was to be in sharing the running of the community health programme. For that I had two capable, competent colleagues with whom to work. One was a Rwandan called Veronique, who had been involved in the setting up of the project some years ago, and the other was Anatolie, who had been the social worker at Gahini Hospital for the past two years.

I was very much the new one, with little experience

of community work, but was eager to learn. My role as Tear Fund overseas worker was to work alongside and train a national colleague, with the aim of leaving the project running in her hands by the end of my four-year contract. But I clearly had much more to learn from them in the beginning than I could hope to pass on.

Everyone was very patient with me, spending many hours sitting round a rough wooden table in our office as I tried to grasp the running of the project, the geographical and political breakdown of the area we covered, and attempted to remember some of the names of the fifty or so health workers in our extended team. Our catchment area was the Commune of Rukara with a population of some 50,000. We were much more fortunate than most rural communes in that Rukara had a hospital as well as a small health centre, but many people still had to walk miles for their medical care. Part of the community health programme involved taking the care to where the people were – holding monthly clinics in remote health posts.

My immediate role, it seemed, was to be that of chauffeuse and midwife, both of whom they had been without since Jill's accident almost a year ago. A slight problem, however, was that they had also been without a vehicle for the past year – and still were. As a large part of our work involved travelling twice weekly to health posts some miles away, I could see this was going to be tricky to say the least. It meant that for the next year, until we had our own community health pick-up truck, we were dependent upon begging and borrowing our expatriate colleagues' vehicles, and adjusting to fit in with their schedules. Not very easy – and certainly not conducive to good relationships!

I loved the trips out to these distant health posts. There were usually four of us who travelled together – Anatolie, Veronique, myself, and Gatera, the rather rotund and slow-moving vaccinator. The posts themselves were only empty brick and cement buildings, so we had to take all our equipment with us: pressure cookers of sterilised syringes and needles (re-used so many times that they had become quite blunt), a thermos of cold vaccines, foldable tables and stools, a mattress for the pregnant ladies to lie on, weighing scales for the babies, and much more.

'Has anyone remembered to put in the water today?' Anatolie could always be relied upon to think of everything. There was no water where we were going, and handling dozens of grubby, squirming children throughout the day could be quite a messy business. So a small, mud-stained jerrycan of water was brought and squeezed into the last remaining space in our vehicle, together with a bar of soap and towel.

Finally, before setting off, watched by a group of intrigued youngsters hoping to catch a free ride on the back of the laden vehicle, one of the team members took their turn to pray. 'Father, we thank you for the health and strength you have given us, and for this opportunity to serve you in our work. You know that the day ahead of us is a difficult one, and we know that we need your help in it. Please protect us over these bad roads as we travel in this metal-thing-which-has-no-wisdom [as they often referred to the car!] and give wisdom to our driver. Please help us to be patient with the women and children who will be waiting for us, and help us to show your love to them in everything we do and say. Amen.'

It was lovely to drive off into the countryside, leaving

the hospital behind for the day. The farthest away
health post was at a place called Juru, meaning 'heaven'
– a forty-five-minute drive when the roads were dry,
but anything up to an hour and a half when the rain
had turned the roads into a mud bath. A good part of
that journey took us alongside the edge of the Akagera
National Wildlife Park. The acute shortage of land
space in Rwanda meant that the local population were
forced to cultivate their crops right up to the edge of
the Park. There was no fence to stop trespassers enter-
ing or wild animals coming out, so those who lived
nearest often had their crops destroyed by stray buffalo.

It was an extremely beautiful journey. One moment
the road would be winding through intensely cultivated valleys, densely covered with lush green banana
plantations; the next we would be chugging to the top
of a stony hill with tremendous views across the hills
and valleys for miles on every side.

Although initially I was unfamiliar with the areas, I
quickly learnt that we must be nearing the health post
as we passed more and more women walking barefoot
along the road. Some were alone, some in groups, but
each one was dressed in brightly coloured cloths and
was either heavily pregnant, or else carried a small
child strapped firmly to her back.

The health post at Juru stood alone on the top of a
hill, exposed to the wind and rain. While we unloaded
and set up our equipment, the women spent a few
minutes working with their hoes and scythes on the
small piece of land that surrounded the building,
digging out the weeds and trimming the grass on the
path. It was hot, back-breaking work. Most of these
women had been up since the first light, around five o'
clock, to spend a couple of hours in their own fields

before walking for miles to reach the clinic. Yet they never complained, and were grateful that they did not have to make the much longer journey to Gahini.

The session at the clinic began with an animated talk by Anatolie on some aspect of health – on this occasion the prevention of worms; another time perhaps how to make a home-made water filter, or the importance of spacing out the size of a family. (Rwanda was the most densely populated country in Africa.) I could understand very little of what was said, but I could tell by the lively exchange of questions and ideas that her teaching was being thought-provoking to say the least!

During the teaching session the women sat around on the uneven stone floor, somewhere between fifty and one hundred of them, all crowded in together out of the strong rays of the sun. But as soon as it was over, they were up and moving, jostling and pushing, some queuing to have their babies weighed, others trying to be first to have their babies vaccinated, and some hoping to obtain secretly their next supply of contraceptive pills. The use of contraception was actively promoted by the government, but exaggerated rumours of unpleasant side-effects of contraception, together with strong religious and traditional beliefs in the country, resulted in all forms of family planning being viewed with much suspicion and criticism. Those who were brave enough to try did so secretly to avoid hurtful criticism from friends and neighbours – and even at times from their husbands.

Outside one of the little rooms was a rapidly growing queue of heavily pregnant ladies waiting for me. My task was to try to hold an antenatal clinic with my almost non-existent command of the language. The country women spoke only Kinyarwandan, and the rest of our team, with whom I communicated for the time being in French, were too busy in their own jobs to spare the time to sit with me. We agreed that I should call on one of them if I was completely stuck.

So, armed with my little list of 'useful phrases' that Trisha had taught me and I had been practising for days, I called the ladies in, one at a time. Not surprisingly, my mangled attempts to ask a woman to lie on the mattress, or to sit up, often met with a totally blank stare. But what seemed to me to be much more amazing was the discovery that *sometimes*, when I produced the same combination of strange sounds, it clearly meant something to the hearer, and she would lie down or sit up in response!

In these early weeks I frequently had to call for the help of an interpreter, but as time went by it was always a huge encouragement to me to find my vocabulary growing and to be able to communicate more and more with the women.

It was well into the afternoon when I opened the door to my little room and found to my enormous relief that there were no more pregnant women waiting outside. It had been a long, hot and noisy day. The screams of the children as they were vaccinated in the little room next door to mine made it difficult to listen accurately to the foetal hearts through my little 'trumpet' stethoscope. And the wind had been whistling outside for most of the day, causing the corrugated tin roofing to rattle and bang, and whipping up the dust in miniature whirlwinds. I felt absolutely filthy, and it seemed a long time since breakfast.

I was just stuffing my rolled-up, dusty mattress into its plastic bag when a young woman walked in with a baby in her arms. Her eyes were sad and weary. I did not have to look hard at the emaciated, sickly child to realise that it was seriously ill. At that moment, Anatolie appeared at the doorway.

'Her child is sick and she wants you to treat it,' she said.

'*Me*?' I exclaimed, somewhat taken aback. 'But I'm not a *doctor*! I can't treat this child. She'll need to bring it to the hospital.'

With that, I looked outside and realised that there were others waiting, all sitting on the dusty stone floor. There was an elderly man, bent over a stick, with a painful-looking swollen foot; another mother with a small frightened girl with sunken eyes; two women with their coloured cloths pulled up over their heads, shivering.

'What are these people waiting for?' I asked Anatolie.

'They're all sick. They've come for medicines.'

I was amazed. 'But what makes them think I can help them? I mean, I'm not trained to diagnose illnesses or dispense drugs. I'm a nurse, not a doctor. Anatolie, please can you tell them that. They'll have to come to Gahini.'

Anatolie explained something to them, and they eventually wandered off looking very disappointed. All, that is, except the lady with the very ill baby. She had negotiated a lift with us back to Gahini. So, with a bit of rearranging, we managed to squeeze her into our already overcrowded car.

It was during the journey back in the car that I discovered that my predecessor, Jill, used to take a big wooden box of medicines with her on these trips, and regularly treated those who were sick. It was only natural, therefore, that the local people should assume that I would do the same. On top of that, in my hospital work I was discovering that Rwandan nurses learn, as part of their training, to diagnose and treat common minor ailments. In fact, many small health clinics are run entirely by nurses.

Of those who came today because they were sick, I wondered to myself, how many would be prepared to make the long journey to Gahini to see the doctor? How would I feel having to walk all those miles if I was feverish, weak and shivery? *And* if I was pregnant on top of that? I then decided I should look inside the medicine box that Jill had used.

The trouble was that in my training as a nurse it had been ingrained into me that drugs were only prescribed by a doctor. If I were now to use my own initiative to diagnose the problem, and then prescribe and dispense medicines, what might be the outcome? I had a kind of lurking fear that some senior nurse would appear from behind a bush and come thundering down on me, and I would be struck off the nursing register. Or worse still, maybe my treatment would go horribly wrong and the patient would sue me!

Yet the reality of the situation here in rural Gahini was that there was no senior nurse to come breathing down my neck. *I* was the senior nurse now! I discussed it with Rob over the next few days and we decided that if I limited myself to treating a small number of common diseases, there was actually very little that could go wrong.

Malaria, for example, was extremely common in Rwanda and relatively easy to treat in most cases. To ignore it, though, could have drastic consequences, particularly for a pregnant woman – possibly killing her unborn baby or causing it to be born prematurely, or even resulting in the death of the mother herself.

Those two shivering women I turned away probably had malaria and might not make it to the hospital, but had I given them the initial course of treatment, at least they would have had a fairly good chance of recovering. It was dawning on me that I would have to rethink some of my traditional ideas of nursing in the UK, and begin to adapt to a very different situation in Rwanda.

Treating the sick was of course important, but the whole purpose of the community health work was in the prevention of disease; and that was why I had come. It was quick and easy to give a course of worm medicine to a child with a bloated stomach and diarrhoea, but without addressing the cause of his problem – where the worms came from – he will simply come back again and again for the same medicine, using up his family's precious money, and in the meantime growing weaker and weaker.

However, enforcing new ideas, as had sometimes been the practice in the past, was not the answer. People had to be convinced of the need to change and of the personal benefits of an improved standard of health. When visiting the homes of particularly problematic families, for example, I was sometimes mystified to see the state of their pit latrines. The owner would lead us to a tumbledown structure some distance away from the house, where there was clearly no path, and the 'long drop' was obviously not in use, and announce with pride, 'Here it is.'

So why the pride in this latrine if no one used it, and as a result the whole family suffered chronic worm infestations? Anatolie explained. 'You see, in the time of the Belgians it was the law that everyone had to have a pit latrine, otherwise they would be fined 5,000 francs. So everyone dug a shallow hole and built a little shed over the top, but many folk never used it because they could see no reason to do so.' Therefore it had been a quick way of enforcing superficial changes, but had no impact on the health of the population. Our aim, however, would be to work alongside the population – discussing, teaching and showing by example the benefits they would gain by improvements in their health.

This was where the health workers, or ASBs (Agents Sanitaire de Base) as they were called, came into their own. These were local men and women, chosen by their own communities, and trained by us in the very basics of preventative health. They were expected to visit regularly the families in their neighbourhood, chat with them to find out what particular health difficulties they were experiencing, and then help them to find workable solutions to their problems. They would offer advice – perhaps explaining the importance of boiling water before drinking it, or of spacing out their pregnancies, or of growing fruit and vegetables to supplement their children's diet. The ASBs checked to see who had not brought their child to the vaccination session and then visited the family to find out why.

Some ASBs, though, were less committed than others, and seemed to think that all the community's health problems could be solved over a few gourds of the local home brew down in the nearby pub. Their own homes fell far short of the ideal, so any advice they had to offer carried little weight.

I found it hard to get used to being in a position of management, particularly when there were questions of discipline to be addressed. Anatolie and Veronique were happy to give advice and explanation, but always deferred to me for a decision. Perhaps simply because I was white, they felt I carried more authority.

Work took up a lot of my time, but there were new experiences on the home front too. Having spent six weeks with Etienne's and Emeralde's family, I moved in to a little house on my own. It was sad to move away from the warm hospitality of the extended family, but being a true Brit I was actually quite glad of some privacy and peace and quiet! I now had the luxury of running water most of the time, and electricity for two to three hours in the evenings when the hospital generator was working.

However, the novelty that I had most difficulty in adjusting to was having staff working for me personally. I was given a housegirl, and told I would also need to employ a gardener and a night guard! What on earth would I do with three staff working for me? I quickly discovered, though, that without Grace as my housegirl, and Matayo in the garden, I would have had no time for work; and as a single girl living alone, a night guard was essential for security.

Every task was so time-consuming: hand-washing the clothes, cleaning, cooking, carrying water, cutting the grass with a scythe. Initially I wondered if I could do some of these tasks myself after work, but as there were barely two hours of daylight in the evening – and those were frequently taken up with unexpected visitors – I soon realised that that was not an option either.

It eased my conscience to discover that most families, Rwandans as well as *Bazungu*, had help at home, either from the extended family or employees. And everyone would have thought it incomprehensible had I not had anyone to help me. None the less, it still felt strange.

Grace, though, was much more than a housegirl for me. At times I was quite lonely in my own little place, and having Grace around was good fun. Conversation was not very adventurous at lunch-times, but she was always terribly patient with my attempts to speak Kinyarwanda, and we had lots of laughs together.

As time went by and my language improved, I began to get to know her a little better. Her parents had both died when she was young, and she now lived with her older brother, his wife and their eight children. However, her sister-in-law treated her badly, and only tolerated her at home because Grace gave most of her salary for the running of the house. Grace never complained, but sometimes her sad face gave away her secret, and she would shed a few tears.

From my balcony I could see the path she took to work – down a steep hill, across the valley, and up the hill on the Gahini side. It took nearly an hour each way, but she was very rarely late, however heavy the rain or strong the sun.

Grace had a very good friend called Beatrice who also worked as a housegirl, just over the hedge from us with Lionel and Mary. They were like Little and Large, Beatrice being tall and rather generously proportioned, and Grace being short and petite. And they laughed nearly all the time. They were both keen Christians and were always involved in any local Scripture Union (SU) event, usually working hard behind the scenes in the kitchens. On one such occasion, our local SU group, which I had recently joined, was holding a series of meetings in Gahini. Over two hundred people were coming from all around, and they all had to be fed and housed.

The preparation started well in advance as local SU members volunteered contributions to the food – perhaps a basket of beans, or a stick of bananas, or bag of peanuts. Then there were huge bundles of firewood to be carried on our heads up the hill to the church. Yet the bit I most enjoyed was the cooking: sitting on the grass chatting with Grace and Beatrice and other local women, peeling hundreds of sweet potatoes, washing bucketfuls of rice and stoking the fires.

There was often a tendency at big events to treat the *Bazungu* as especially honoured guests, which I found hard to accept. For me it was much more fun, at times such as this, to be able to join in with the local girls, sharing in the menial tasks.

Not long after moving into my own home I was joined by a new companion – a puppy called Isla. I had acquired her from Lionel and Mary after a stray bitch had landed herself on their doorstep and given birth to nine puppies.

Isla was great company to have around. She had a tiny mud hut with a grass roof which Matayo built for her beside the outside sheds, but whenever I was around she stayed near me. Her favourite spot in the house was curled up in a ball on the bottom of the bookshelf in the sitting-room!

One of the lovely things about dogs is their faithfulness and allegiance to their owners. Sometimes, after an especially difficult or frustrating day at work, I would return home feeling less than enthusiastic about life in Gahini. But with Isla there to greet me, thrusting her muddy paws all over me and jumping up and down whining with excitement, it was impossible to stay discouraged for long. And it was a great life for a dog. With so few cars around, Isla was able to have a free run of the hill, and often came out for walks with me whenever I went to visit friends after work.

Visiting. The word really needs to be spelt with a capital V, as it was such an important part of the culture in the countryside. Being a very sociable people, most would consider it an honour to receive a visitor, however unexpected, and so they presumably thought I would view it the same way. However, for me, coming from a culture where plans are made weeks in advance (and then only after consulting a diary!), and where telephones provide an immediate link to warn of changes, it was not always easy to adjust. It always seemed to be when I was feeling at my most tired and unsociable that visitors would turn up on the doorstep. It would have been quite unacceptable not to invite them in, at least for a short while, and chat over a cup of tea and some bananas. And so time and again, my own plans had to be shelved for yet another evening.

It was not just friends who came to visit either. The scourge of AIDS in Rwanda, together with minimal rainfall and subsequent poor harvests, meant that there were many needy people around. It was not uncommon to come home from work and find a bedraggled-looking woman with a baby on her back and a mal-nourished child in tow, begging for food at the back door.

One day I found three young children, perhaps aged about twelve, ten and eight years old, standing by my back door with bundles of firewood. 'They've been there all day,' Matayo told me. 'They want to sell you their firewood.' Matayo was the expert in knowing the going prices, so I asked his advice. 'It's a bit expensive,' he commented, 'but they are poor folk. I know their family. It's up to you if you want to buy it.'

I chatted a little to the children and discovered that they had left home early in the morning to avoid the worst of the sun, and had walked for over an hour with these heavy loads on their heads. They had not eaten all day, and were about to make the long journey home. So I gave them some sweet tea, and a plate of bread and bananas which they devoured ravenously – and of course I bought their firewood. However, the next morning they were back with more firewood – and every day after that until eventually I had to ask them to come less often. There was a limit to the amount of firewood I could use!

One Saturday evening their mother came to visit me, and she was amazed and concerned to discover that I had no one to help me in the house in the evenings. 'You could give me your girl,' I laughed, referring to her twelve-year-old daughter. It was not uncommon for a young sister or cousin to be given to a single professional or newly married couple to help them at home, but I was of course joking.

The next day was Sunday – my one long lie-in of the week. There was a loud knock at the door at 7 a.m. Oh no! It was the mother – together with her daughter who was clutching a crumpled plastic carrier bag containing a few of her personal possessions.

'Here you are. I've brought her to live with you. She'll work well for you.'

It took me some time to explain my way out of that one, and it was definitely the last time I would make a joke with someone I did not know well!

When I first went to Rwanda at the end of the 1980s, I understood it to be one of the more stable and safe countries of Africa. I had heard of violent uprisings in previous years, but for the past decade or so it had seemed to be a country at peace, and with a growing economy and infrastructure.

But as was the case in many countries in the continent of Africa around that time, Rwanda was experiencing significant changes on the political front with the introduction of many new political parties, both inside and outside the country; in 1959 and the early 1960s, many thousands of Rwandans, mostly from the minority Tutsi tribe, were massacred following the transfer of power from a Tutsi monarchy to a Hutu-controlled state. Others managed to escape and fled to neighbouring countries, particularly Uganda and Burundi, where they had been living ever since.

Attempts to reintegrate the hundreds of thousands of exiled Rwandans back into their country had made no progress, and a section of these refugees had recently formed themselves into a powerful political and military force, the Rwandan Patriotic Front (RPF). Many within Rwanda feared that the RPF might be planning a massive military return.

By late summer 1990, Rwanda was preparing for the visit of the Pope. Rumours circulated, suggesting that his visit might be the pretext by which these exiled Rwandans would re-enter their country, ostensibly to see him, and then stage a coup from the inside. This possibility was talked about in hushed tones, but our sleepy little village seemed a long way from the capital of Kigali, where any trouble would be more likely to take place. 'Anyway it'll probably not come to anything,' I wrote to my parents on 30 September 1990. 'So I wouldn't worry about it.'

My thinking at that time was more taken up with the news that a sister project to ours (the Gahini environmental health project), which had collapsed a couple of years back, was about to be resurrected with a new director. 'I'm hoping that we'll be able to work closely together,' I continued in that same letter. 'We'll be concentrating on the health side of things; they'll be involved in setting up projects, advising on agriculture, working for clean water supplies, etc., and hopefully take a lead in spiritual things since two of them are Christians.'

The new project director was to be a young Rwandan Christian who had just finished studying in Kenya; his name was Charles Bilinda.

3

Marriage to Charles

On 1 October 1990, a British friend arrived in Rwanda to visit me for a holiday. She was the first friend who had come out and I was really looking forward to taking some time off to travel around the country with her. When I returned to Gahini that evening, after collecting her from Kigali airport, we were told the news: Rwanda had been invaded.

So the rumours that had been circulating were true. The RPF had crossed Rwanda's northern border with Uganda and was advancing on Kigali. Within just two days the country had come to a complete standstill. All but essential services at the hospital ground to a halt as we rapidly started to run out of fuel. A twenty-four hour curfew prevented all travel anywhere. We could only watch with binoculars from our balconies as convoys of army trucks and bus-loads of soldiers thundered up and down the road to the border; and listen as helicopters circled menacingly low over Gahini and the lake. Understandably, tensions were running very high.

A few days after it all began, army trucks arrived at the hospital, and two of the hospital staff were taken away. We were all shaken, and the rumours began to fly around: 'Were they accomplices of the RPF? Who would be next to go?'

But no one else did go from the hospital. In Kigali, however, a night of shooting resulted in house to house searches, and thousands of Tutsis were rounded up on suspicion of being RPF accomplices. Many died of dehydration while being held for days in the city's football stadium, without water and in the burning sun.

Having no telephone or two-way radio in Gahini, and with travel impossible, we were unable to make any contact with the outside world for some ten days. However, eventually the curfew was reduced, and we were able to persuade our local *Bourgemeistre* (the Mayor) that the hospital could no longer function without fuel. He provided me with some official papers permitting me to travel, and I set off together with the hospital administrator for Kibungo town, some fifty kilometres away.

It was slow going as I was extremely nervous, and we had to stop at every stick or pile of leaves on the road in case it was a road block. An abandoned car in the middle of the road, peppered with bullet holes, served as a very effective reminder that the soldiers on the road blocks were to be taken seriously. In Kibungo, as well as buying essential supplies there for the hospital, I was able to phone Kigali and the UK. It was a huge relief for our families to hear that we were all alive and well.

As expatriates and living in the countryside, we personally did not appear to be in any immediate risk. However, the general insecurity within Rwanda, together with the lack of communication between Gahini and the outside world, meant that we were strongly advised to evacuate. Initially we went to Kigali, but tensions there were running so high that some of us felt it wise to leave for a time and go to Kenya.

It was heartbreaking. We just had time to pack a few things, and pray with some of our Rwandan friends who had come to say goodbye. Our leaving was an ominous sign for them. Was it because we knew something of what was to come? Were things going to get worse? Yet they accepted that we had to go and there was not the slightest trace of resentment in their prayers as they cried to the Lord for our safety on the journey into Kigali.

But our hearts were heavy. How would we ever be able to look them in the eye again, having abandoned them in this time of need? Would we ever come back again?

Over the next few weeks the situation did calm down considerably, and all the expatriate staff were gradually able to return. However, things were different now.

Travel was still severely restricted, and obtaining weekly travel permits for the cars was time-consuming. We had only just finalised the purchase of a brand-new Toyota pick-up for the community health programme, but as much of our catchment area bordered the Akagera National Wildlife Park where many RPF soldiers were still thought to be, we could not use it much. These were no-go areas.

Politics was now the main topic of conversation, but it was always discussed quietly, with furtive glances around to see who might be listening. No one would share openly their true allegiances for fear of reprisals.

The RPF had taken a large section in the north of the

country, causing hundreds of thousands of Rwandans to be displaced into huge makeshift camps. The nearest of these camps was only thirty or so kilometres north of Gahini. On the roads around us it was not unusual to see clusters of shabbily dressed men and women, their few belongings balanced carefully on their heads, skinny bedraggled children in tow. They had come in search of a little food to eke out the meagre rations they were receiving in the camps. It was a pitiful sight.

As there was now no public transport at all, I was always guaranteed company on the days when I travelled to Kigali. People had no way of finding out what had happened to their friends and relatives other than by visiting or by sending notes by hand, so they were always desperate for lifts. On the road between Gahini and Kigali there were six road blocks manned by soldiers. It must have been a terribly boring job, I thought, just sitting around most of the day, as the difficulty in obtaining travel permits and fuel meant there were now even fewer vehicles on the road.

Often the soldiers would be keen to chat, and although they did not insist on a bribe, they were always interested to see what we had in the car that we could share with them. Most of them could read, so I seized the opportunity to hand out a New Testament in Kinyarwandan whenever possible. There was great prestige in owning a book, and since they had so little to do all day, there was a good chance the soldiers might actually read it!

It was during this time of uncertainty and tension that Charles Bilinda came to live in Gahini. The environmental health project to which he had originally been assigned by the diocese never got off the ground, so instead he was allocated to the Petit Seminaire, the local church secondary school, as an English teacher. It was a job to which he was well suited.

Charles did not know when his birthday was. All he knew was that he was born sometime in November 1959 as his parents walked from North to South Rwanda, fleeing the massacres of Tutsis that ravaged their home area. Most of his primary schooling was in Rwanda, but at the age of fifteen his parents sent him to Uganda to live with an aunt in order to finish his schooling. It was difficult at that time for children of Tutsi parents to reach a good standard of education within Rwanda.

While in Uganda Charles completed secondary schooling and went on to gain a teaching qualification. Two years of teaching in Kigali was then followed by the fulfilment of a longing of many years to train as a pastor. He spent three years in Kenya studying for a Bachelor of Divinity degree, before returning to Rwanda in September 1990 to work with the Kigali diocese of the Episcopal Church of Rwanda.

Charles threw himself into his new job with great enthusiasm and energy, and developed a firm friendship with the headmaster, an equally committed and hard-working pastor of the Episcopal Church. There were not many Rwandans around with such outgoing personalities, and who spoke fluent English, so Charles quickly endeared himself to my neighbours, Lionel and Mary. I often used to find him up at their house, chatting and laughing with them on the balcony.

'I could see you two together, you know,' Lionel said to me one evening after Charles had gone home. 'I could imagine you living out here long term, sending your kids to the local primary school.' I laughed. What a ridiculous idea! Lionel was always the romantic, the matchmaker. Well, let him speculate, I thought.

But as time went by Charles visited more and more. He was always keen to join in whatever was going on, and we all had lots of laughs – whether it was watching his enthusiastic attempts at Scottish country dancing at a Burns Supper outside in the moonlight, or seeing the look of triumph on his face when, after mastering the art of tossing a pancake, he eventually succeeded in catching it again in the frying pan!

One of his desires in life was to learn to swim, and the lake at the bottom of our hill seemed the ideal opportunity to fulfil this ambition. However, our nearest lakeside clearing was regularly used by the local schoolchildren for collecting water and washing – and it would be much too embarrassing for the local teacher to be seen floundering around in the water! So we found an alternative, and from time to time Sue (a short-term British nurse living with me) and I would squeeze on to the back of Charles's motorbike and drive a few miles round the lake to a much quieter spot. With typical enthusiasm and fun, Charles rose to this new challenge, and squeezed his rather round tummy into a patched-up old inner car tyre, which served as a rubber ring.

Charles had never been taught how to swim, but what he lacked in skill he more than made up for in determination. The look of total concentration on his screwed-up face as he bobbed up and down, thrashing madly at the water, had Sue and I so doubled up in laughter that we could hardly keep ourselves afloat, let alone offer any instruction.

Although swimming may not have been his 'forte', he certainly left us far behind when it came to riding his motorbike. Part of his job included inspecting primary schools within the diocese of Kigali, and for that he'd been given the motorbike. Some of the schools were located in very remote areas, over rough and muddy roads, so he quickly developed new and useful skills in riding the motorbike.

He took great care of his vehicle, keeping it clean, polished and regularly serviced. And long after some of his colleagues' motorbikes had bitten the dust through rough use and neglect, Charles's bike still looked brand-new. He even kept it in the sitting-room at night – not perhaps as strange as it may sound, for the floor was cement and regularly washed out, and a motorbike was such a prized possession that had it been left outside, it would likely not have still been there in the morning.

Yet it was not only his motorbike that Charles took care of. Considering that he was a young man living alone (and men in Rwanda are not normally remotely concerned with domestic matters), I was always amazed to see how neat and clean his house was, and what lovely meals he produced (although perhaps his houseboy was largely responsible for the latter!). Even his outside pit latrine was spotless.

During the later months of 1991 our friendship was beginning to deepen, but developing a relationship in this culture was not easy – particularly in the claustrophobic atmosphere of Gahini. Courtships just did not seem to exist in Rwandan culture. A young man would make a calculated decision (usually based on trusted recommendation) about a prospective wife, and then simply ask her to marry him. The main criteria would usually be that she could cook, was reasonably good looking, and would make a good mother and homemaker. A decision to marry would be made without the two people necessarily knowing one another well.

Because Charles had lived much of his life outside of Rwanda, he was able to combine this purely practical approach with a more Western romantic attitude. There were also big issues for Charles and me to work through, particularly as we began to think through the implications of a cross-cultural marriage. For both of us, our hearts were in Africa – and Rwanda in particular – which would probably mean spending the best part of our lives there. However, I would not necessarily be working indefinitely for a British-based agency, or even earning a salary at all, so we would both have to survive on Charles's salary – which at the time was about one-quarter of mine. Ultimately that would mean fewer and fewer trips back home to the UK, and seeing less and less of my family and friends there. That would be very hard for me.

There would be the question of schooling for any children we might have (the local village school did not have a particularly high standard of education). There were issues of roles and responsibilities, and the question of our respective families' views on a marriage. There was so much to consider; this was certainly not a decision to be rushed into or taken lightly.

And to make matters even more complicated, Charles felt strongly that our friendship should not be publicly seen and known at this early stage. It was not easy for us to get to know one another well in secret, but he was insistent. I was aware that a growing friendship (if it was even acknowledged) between two young people would rarely be known publicly, except to a few close friends, but it was some time before I was to discover the significance of this custom.

*

During the months following the RPF invasion in October 1990, Rwanda became increasingly unstable. Any further movement by the RPF in the north brought about reprisals elsewhere in the country, particularly against Tutsis, who were accused of being RPF accomplices – or at least that was the official line. In the myriad of rumours that were circulating wildly, it was virtually impossible to determine the truth.

In March 1992 news came through of a massacre in an area not far from Kigali, where Charles's family home was. It was an area with a higher than average proportion of Tutsis, and many hundreds were reported to have been slaughtered. No one seemed to know the cause, but – as with most riots and uprisings in those days – the old and new political parties blamed each other.

One week later Charles popped in to see me having just returned from a trip to Kigali. I wrote about his visit in my diary:

> He brought news not only of a bomb blast at the taxi station killing an estimated forty people, but much worse. His brother, wife and five kids were all killed. It's one thing to hear of numbers announced on the news. But these are all people, the nearest and dearest of one dear to me. It would be as if my own sister, husband and five kids were wiped out in one fell swoop ... A car accident would be bad enough, but to think that they might have been burnt to death or hacked up. It just makes me sick.

The news had been brought to him by a reliable source, so he had no reason to doubt it. Yet only a few weeks later, when the roads in Bugesera were cleared and he was able to ride there on his motorbike, he discovered that all of his family were still alive. It had been yet another false rumour, underlining for me again the difficulty in knowing who to trust, who is telling the truth.

Throughout this time, when not overwhelmed by the circumstances around us, Charles and I continued to talk through the possibility of marriage. By the end of the summer of 1992, after much prayer, heart-searching and discussion, we were convinced that we should go ahead. As we would likely be spending most of our lives in Rwanda, we decided to hold the wedding locally, as opposed to in the UK, and to aim for the end of the year. These months passed very quickly as there was so much to do, and for a while the troubles of the country took more of a back seat in my thinking.

In traditional Rwandan culture a marriage would take months, with umpteen negotiations taking place between the close family friends who represented the groom's and the bride's families. However, we condensed it down to two days, as tended to be the custom in modern-day Rwanda – 30 December for the traditional ceremonies in Gahini, and 2 January for the church wedding in Kigali.

'Look! He's arrived. Doesn't he look funny with those clothes!' There were about ten of us crowded round the tiny window in what had been my bedroom at Etienne's and Emeralde's house, watching for Charles's arrival. My own parents had arrived in Rwanda just the day before, but they were able to sit back and enjoy themselves because Etienne and Emeralde had taken on their full responsibility as my Rwandan 'parents', hosting the ceremonies as if I was their real daughter.

And that was no mean task. They had been busy preparing for weeks, involving many of the neighbours and friends from near and far. Weddings were big community events, and most of the local population would turn up hoping for some food or drink, whether invited or not. Moreover, the marriage of a Rwandan to a *Muzungu* (white person) was almost unheard of in our country area, so everyone was curious to see what would happen.

The official ceremonies had begun in the morning, in the Rukara local administrative offices, some 12 kilometres from Gahini. In the presence of the *Bourgemeistre* and a room full of friends, we repeated our vows and 'signed' with our thumb prints on umpteen forms. Then it was back to Gahini in separate cars for the negotiations.

Traditionally the girlfriends of the bride waited inside during this next part of the proceedings. So we crowded into the small hot and stuffy room and waited for what seemed like ages, peeping through the window as the guests arrived and searched for a seat.

There must have been around two to three hundred folk outside in the garden, squeezed into every possible little space. A large wooden structure with a tarpaulin and banana-leaf canopy had been specially constructed, so that at least some of the guests had shade from the strong sun. Dozens more peered in from outside the garden hedge and crowded round the gate, pushing and shoving to get a view of the proceedings inside.

There was certainly plenty to see. Charles was wearing traditional white cloths, rarely seen in these modern times. One was wrapped around his waist and came down almost to his ankles (but short enough to reveal his less-than-traditional bright new baseball boots!), and the other was pinned over his shoulder. I and the girls accompanying me also wore cloths of a similar traditional style, but more brightly coloured.

The representative from Charles's family was the first to speak. He had come, he explained with much ceremony and hilarity, to seek a wife for this son of the family, and the wife's name was Lesley. Well, that would be difficult, our representative replied, pretending that there was no such girl living here! But with a twinkle in his eye, he suggested offering some alternative brides from which Charles could choose.

With that, my eleven-year-old niece, Joanna, was paraded outside together with the five-year-old and three-year-old daughters of a good friend. This brought peels of laughter and applause from the guests, but the suitor was not satisfied, and so the bargaining continued.

Eventually our representative confessed that I was indeed in the house, and so it was our turn to come out, a line of brightly dressed young ladies, greeting each representative of Charles's family in turn. Fortunately Charles made the right choice and I took my seat beside him. There followed a lively display of singing and dancing, an exchange of gifts, and then ... the cows!

To the delight of the crowds, two young cows were brought into the yard and trotted around nervously. According to tradition a cow had to be offered by Charles's family to my family, and the other was there to keep it company! An elderly cow 'expert', summoned to examine our one, pronounced it fit and well, and proceeded to perform an energetic song and dance in praise of the cow and of me – and all, it seemed, in the same breath! Needless to say, Mum and Dad were unwilling to suggest to Sabena (the Belgian airline with which they flew) that they might like to include a cow as part of their luggage, so it was to be looked after by my Rwandan 'parents' instead.

As soon as the celebrations were over Charles was due to go to Kigali to finalise arrangements for the church wedding. However, there had been further riots and demonstrations in Kigali, so he was delayed for two days because all the main roads were closed. And that was not the only problem. We had booked our reception in the Horizons Hotel, a beautiful setting on top of one of the many hills overlooking the city. The fact that it belonged to the president's family was of no relevance to us, until we were told, two days before our wedding was due to take place, that the president's son was to be married on the same day as us and that his reception was to be held at the Horizons Hotel!

So Charles left for Kigali two days before our wedding, wondering if he might have to begin all over again looking for a place for our reception. On top of all this, when my parents, sisters and niece arrived, one of their suitcases did not turn up. Unfortunately, it happened to be the suitcase that contained two of the bridesmaids' dresses. 'Oh don't worry,' the airline official had told us. 'This often happens. The plane must have been too full. They'll put it on the next one. It'll be here on Friday.'

Friday? But we were getting married on Saturday!

Sure enough, when we arrived in Kigali on Saturday morning, there was the suitcase, and there were the bridesmaids' dresses. So while the rest of us changed into our wedding clothes, my sister Sheila hurriedly took up the hems and ironed the dresses.

Compared to the preparations, the service and the

reception afterwards went remarkably smoothly. The president's son had apparently chosen to have his reception elsewhere, so ours went ahead without further hitch. More speeches and more food, prepared by Charles's sister, Diane, and her helpers. And more strange sorghum brew.

'It's an experience you can't miss,' I whispered to my niece Joanna, as to her horror the four bridesmaids were summoned to the communal clay pot in the centre of the hall. 'You have to lift the wooden straw up a little bit, so you don't suck up the sludge on the bottom, but not too far so you don't get the froth and bits floating on the top. And then you spend the next ten minutes chewing the bits of grain that got stuck in your teeth. Enjoy it!' Judging by the expression on her face as she returned to her seat, it was an experience she could happily have lived without!

We had a one-night honeymoon in the hotel before returning to Gahini to our third and final reception – this time for all the local people, hospital staff, and ASBs who had not been able to come to the main wedding.

However, if we thought that was the end of the social gatherings, and that now we would be able to rest and recover, we were very much mistaken. There were still more traditions to be seen to, and most of these seemed to involve entertaining massive crowds of visitors. Weekends were particularly busy, with ten to twenty people descending upon us each Sunday for lunch, and thirty, forty or even fifty coming in the afternoons. During weekdays we were back at work, but that did not stop the visitors in the evenings. We had moved into a larger house immediately after the wedding, but were still trying to find time to arrange our belongings and open wedding presents. I was exhausted!

In the end, we decided to take on an extra housegirl to help us in the evenings, since Grace was only around in the mornings. It worked well to begin with, until we discovered that the new housegirl had been stealing from us. As she angrily denied the proof we had gathered, we had no choice but to sack her. In her revenge, though, she began to spread a rumour that I personally had sacked her because she was having an affair with Charles. I knew it was ridiculous and untrue, but none the less it distressed me that someone would want to spread such malicious rumours about us. I couldn't understand why; Charles explained.

'Do you remember before we were married I told you we had to keep quiet about our relationship until the last minute, when the plans had been made? Well, the reason was this. In Rwanda there are two nasty but very common practices. One is called "kwica ubukwe" [or literally 'to kill a wedding']. The other is called "kwica urugo" [or literally 'to kill a home'].

'There are plenty of people around here who pretend to be our friends, but in fact want to destroy us. Maybe it's because you're white and they think I should have taken a Rwandan wife, or because I have a good job and they're jealous. Or maybe it's a racial thing – I don't know. But if they had known of our plans earlier, they would have tried to stop the wedding going ahead. That was why I told you a long time ago that we had to keep it quiet.

'Well, we're married now, but that doesn't stop them from trying to drive a wedge between us and destroying our home. So be careful. They'll sidle up to you and pretend to be kind to you, but they'll try to poison your

thinking. That's exactly what people are doing by
telling you these tales. Just don't listen to them.'

Charles was right – this rumour was not the first I
had heard. Already it had been reported to me that folk
were saying, 'What's Charles marrying a wrinkled old
woman for?' and 'He only married her for her money,
and she only married him because she was left on the
shelf.'

I felt very upset and bitterly disappointed. From
having been accepted and loved as a single white girl,
I now often found myself on the receiving end of much
criticism and hurtful comments.

Yet not everyone was so judgmental. One Saturday
morning, around eleven o' clock, Charles's brother's
wife arrived at the house totally unexpectedly, together
with her sixteen-year-old son. Her younger son was at
school in Gahini, and lived with us, so I presumed they
had come to visit him. Unfortunately, Charles was
away for the day, but I invited her in and we chatted
over a cup of tea.

After an hour she was showing no signs of moving,
so I nipped through to the kitchen to consult quietly
with Grace. 'Do you think I should ask her to stay for
lunch? Charles won't be back for ages, so there's no
point in her waiting for him.'

Grace had already sussed out the situation. 'This is
an important visit. She's really come to see how you
are getting on, so it's important that you receive her
well. And she couldn't go back all the way to Kigali on
a taxi without you first giving her something to eat.
You go back and chat with her – I'll tell you when
lunch is ready.'

I looked around in the kitchen and realised that
Grace had already taken the initiative to prepare extra

food, so I left her to carry on and went back to the sitting-room. Shortly after, she called us through for lunch. Not only had she prepared a sumptuous meal of several different dishes, but she shared the food with us, keeping the conversation going when I dried up, and then cleared everything up at the end.

My sister-in-law left soon after, reassured and satisfied (I presumed!). I went straight through to the kitchen and gave Grace a big hug. 'You are more precious to me than gold, you know. I could *never* have managed without you.'

In fact, it was a tremendous relief to find that Charles's family were so accepting of me, for this was not what some people had led me to expect. As Charles's two older brothers both lived outside the country, and his father was now elderly, a lot of the responsibility for the support for the extended family fell upon him. Sometimes when a man in such a position marries, his sisters can become resentful since his main responsibilities now lie elsewhere.

But not Charles's sisters; not once did I ever sense any hostility towards me. On the contrary, they welcomed and accepted me as belonging to their family. It felt very good to be part of such a reliable and trustworthy family when so much else around me was uncertain and unpredictable.

4

Increasing Tensions and Insecurity

Travel restrictions following the October 1990 invasion had severely disrupted the community health programme, and for some time we had not been able to make our regular trips to the health clinics. Some of the women in the rural areas managed to walk into Gahini for their antenatal appointments, or to have their babies vaccinated, but most did not. It was a difficult time for them.

Anatolie and I decided that we should use this quieter spell to make a start to an AIDS programme that we had been planning for some time. The third member of our team, Veronique, had been transferred to the nearby health centre at Rukara, so Anatolie and I were now working more closely together.

AIDS was a rapidly growing problem in Rwanda, and it seemed that little was being done to tackle it. In contrast to the West, HIV in Africa is mainly spread by heterosexual intercourse; and infidelity after marriage, and promiscuity before marriage, largely contributed to its rampant spread in Rwanda.

Youngsters often had their first experience of sex in their early to mid teens. For girls from poor homes in particular, the offer from an older man of a piece of clothing, some jewellery, or even in some cases simply a bottle of Fanta or a pen for school, in exchange for sex, was too great a temptation to resist. Their thoughts were only for the immediate, not for the long-term consequences. So we worked out a programme of teaching for classes six, seven and eight in all sixteen primary schools in our area. We felt that if those twelve-to-fifteen-year-olds could be given relevant information about AIDS while still young, then perhaps they might think twice before starting on a life of sexual promiscuity.

Anatolie and I had a lot of fun deciding upon and preparing the programme. Most schooling in Rwanda was very traditional, with much repetition and rote learning, so an hour of animation and variety with puppets, quizzes and colourful posters went down very well with most of the youngsters.

However, some of the teachers were not so convinced, particularly the men. 'You're just trying to spoil our fun. We're going to die sooner or later anyway, so we might as well enjoy ourselves while we can,' was a typical reaction. It became obvious that it was going to take more than a simple teaching programme to convince them.

By 1992, although the political tensions were increasing, travel restrictions had been considerably eased and we were once again able to move around freely within our area, resuming our programme of health clinics and home visits. But there were still other problems to contend with. Very low rainfall had resulted in bad harvests and the people of the countryside were facing yet another threat to their existence: drought. It was hard to bring a message of health and hygiene when people were struggling for their very survival. I wrote about this in my diary: 'Today we went to the clinic at Juru and the sight is sickening. Not just brown and dry everywhere, but fields full of dead, dried, unripe crops – especially sorghum, corn and sunflower. Beans are planted but not growing. The women tell us that their husbands are away for days at a time trying to find food, or to earn some money. It's desperate.'

The constant hunger made people weak and increasingly prone to disease. And yet they had no spare money to buy the medicines so needed to treat their illnesses, and they became even weaker. It was a vicious circle in which they were hopelessly trapped. We wondered what we could do in the face of such widespread need.

A growing number of poor people turned up daily at our house, begging for help – a stark reminder of the gulf between our standard of living and theirs. Charles and I kept chickens, so there was a constant supply of eggs to give to any who came, as well as beans, sugar or whatever else we happened to have around. Yet however much we gave away, however many people we helped, we were still not even scratching the surface of the problem. Also it was hard not to feel constantly guilty because of the relative wealth that we had.

Yet it was not simply a question of material well-being; so often the sad faces of those who came betrayed the emptiness in their lives. They had nothing to live for now, and nothing to look forward to in the future. A bag of food might fill their stomachs for a few days, but it did nothing to fill the vacuum in their hearts.

Did God not have an answer to their problems? Should not I, as a Christian, have some words of comfort or encouragement to share with them from God? But my tongue was still; I had nothing to say. Instead I found myself wondering if God was oblivious to their plight, looking down from his heavenly throne, helpless to intervene.

The truth was that I could not enter into their struggles because I had not at that time experienced any real suffering myself. Nor could I bring any message of hope to them, because I had not even begun to understand God's heart of compassion for the broken and the downtrodden. That was yet to come.

Since our marriage, I had noticed that my relationship with other women was changing. Some, it was true, were less than supportive of me in my new role; but others were beginning to open up to me such as they had not done before. Perhaps they felt that as one of the 'married-women class', I could now understand some of the stresses and difficulties they faced – or, more mundanely, perhaps it was simply that my grasp of the language was improving!

Life for women in Rwanda was very hard. The bulk of the responsibilities for bringing up children, running the home, working in the fields and many other tasks fell on them. Men often spent their days drinking home-brewed beers, and many were unfaithful to their wives – and even physically beat them at times. For the women, there was often little alternative other than to bear their lot quietly.

This was certainly not always the pattern, though. An increasing number of women were finding employment and a degree of independence outside the home, as of course was the case with Anatolie. When her husband was made redundant at work, he resisted the pressure to move and find a new job, because he recognised the value of his wife's role in the community health programme and did not want her to have to leave. It was during the first year of my marriage that my friendship with Anatolie also deepened. I enjoyed spending time with her at work, and greatly appreciated her competence and enthusiasm. And I was especially fond of her two gorgeous little girls.

The youngest, Liloise, had been struggling with poor health ever since her traumatic first few days back in 1989, but Mireille, the older one, was a bundle of health and energy, and was growing into a responsible and sweet six-year-old. Mireille took great pride in being allowed to come and visit me all on her own. Sometimes she would bring some lettuces from their garden; sometimes she came to play with the puppies (Isla had had six!); but sometimes she just came to sit and drink a cup of tea and chat.

Then suddenly Mireille was struck down for the first time in her life with malaria. There were very few who had not suffered from malaria at some time or another; the lucky ones had only a mild dose and recovered well. For others, though, it could be very serious, sometimes even fatal. Over all, malaria caused an enormous loss to the economy of Rwanda in terms of absences from work.

Initially Mireille was lucky; she recovered within a few days. But then she succumbed again only weeks later, and this time had to be hospitalised. It was a tense time for Anatolie and her husband until she finally pulled through. The third time Mireille contracted the illness she was much worse and did not respond to treatment. Everything possible was done for her, but this time she did not recover. We were all devastated, not only over the loss of this vibrant, happy child, but of the tragedy for Anatolie and her husband. Having already had two babies die soon after birth, it was unlikely that she would dare attempt to have any more. Once again, Anatolie bore her pain with amazing strength and patience.

Half of Gahini must have been at Mireille's funeral. Without as much as a tremor in her voice, Anatolie praised God for the six years they had enjoyed the company of this little girl; and she thanked Rob and the hospital staff for all the effort and care they had put into caring for her in her last days. There was not a dry eye around. If I had respected Anatolie before all this happened, I did so even more now. I considered myself privileged to have such a great friend.

Anatolie kept herself apart from all the gossip-mongers around the hospital, and I trusted her opinions. So during our trips out together in the car I would often quiz her about the latest happenings on the political scene. She was a Tutsi, and very anxious about the increasing insecurity in the country, although she would never voice her concerns publicly.

Her husband now had another job teaching maths in the state secondary school in Gahini. It was a large school and many of the pupils were young men aged up to their early twenties. Sometimes I would feel quite nervous if walking past the school buildings in the evenings, particularly after a recent riot in the Petit Seminaire, where Charles taught.

My fears were not unfounded. One day, one of the female pupils went missing, and her colleagues asked for permission to go and look for her. However, they were refused. The following day the girl was found drowned in the lake, and the blame was put on the headmaster and the 'prefet de discipline' for not allowing the search. A riot broke out soon after, and as had been the case in the previous riot, we were once again asked to summon help, the school vehicle having been sabotaged. But this time it did not calm down quickly. The headmaster of the Petit Seminaire was kidnapped, and the headmaster and 'prefet de discipline' of the state school went into hiding.

The latter was a good friend of Charles. He appeared on our doorstep late that night, very frightened, and asked us to hide him. Although conscious that our house was very insecure – a hefty shoulder could easily have broken down the doors – we took him in, and he stayed with us for a week until the troubles died down and the pupils were sent home.

For months we had prayed together every evening, asking the Lord to protect us through the night, then thanking him in the morning for a quiet and safe night. But over that week, I prayed those prayers in much greater earnest than I had done previously.

During this first year of our marriage there were also significant changes taking place within the Church. Kigali diocese, of which we were a part, was to divide into two and we would then come under the new diocese of Kibungo. The two main candidates for bishop were both well suited to the job, competent and godly men. It would be a pleasure to work with either of them.

But the run-up to the election of the bishop became a sordid tale of rumours, counter-rumours and deep divisions between the supporters of the two candidates. Consequently, we found ourselves in a tricky position.

As a pastor and member of the Synod, Charles was entitled to vote, but as both men and their families were good friends of ours, it was very difficult for Charles to know which way to vote. In the end, it was the headmaster of his school who was appointed, and he in turn appointed Charles to the post of diocesan secretary.

Being a new diocese, though, and without the backing of the parent diocese in Kigali (since our new bishop was not the choice of the bishop of Kigali diocese), the two of them found themselves with a huge amount of work on their hands. Charles had been in the habit of working hard from Monday to Saturday, usually from morning till late evening. But now, on top of that he was out all day on Sunday as well, since he had to accompany the new bishop on all his visits to the parishes.

By early 1994, with the tensions in the country having grown to such a point that we lived with our emergency bags packed in case of sudden evacuation, and with so many stresses at work and around us, I felt it was really time we had a holiday. We had not had a rest since our marriage fifteen months previously. It would do us both good, I thought, to get away for a couple of weeks and relax.

Yet Charles saw things differently from me. He had grown up with tensions and crises in the country, and he was generally optimistic about the political situation. A peace agreement had recently been agreed upon in Arusha, Tanzania, which would, among other things, allow the return of Rwandan refugees from neighbouring countries. Many of those refugees were his friends, and he was looking forward to seeing them again, as well as to the changes in the country that their return would bring.

However, he was not oblivious to the current political volatility, and felt it would be unwise to travel far within the country. Nor did he feel it appropriate to take time out at that point for a holiday outside the country. So reluctantly, I decided to go on holiday on my own. My sister Sue agreed to fly out from Scotland and join me in Kenya for ten days, so on 29 March 1994 I flew out of Rwanda.

5

Killing Beyond Belief –
The Genocide Begins

I stretched out my hand from underneath the mosquito net and drew back the curtain a little. 'Hey Sue,' I said. 'It looks gorgeous out there again.'

In fact, there are not many days when the sun does not shine brilliantly on the Mombasa south coast, and even when it does rain, it is still very hot. It is an astoundingly beautiful place – just as it is on picture postcards. Peering through between the tall shady palm trees dotted over the grass, I could see a vast expanse of hot, white sands, edging the rich, royal blue and turquoise waters of the Indian Ocean.

Today we had arranged to go snorkelling. Neither of us knew much about it, but there was no shortage of enthusiastic young Kenyan guides strolling around on the beach looking for customers. We had made a deal with someone called Michael on the previous day; he was to provide the equipment and be our guide for the morning. We had arranged to meet at ten o'clock to allow time to walk out to the reefs and back in low tide. Hiring a boat would have been much more expensive, and not nearly so adventurous. I was really looking forward to our expedition.

Extricating myself from my tangled-up mosquito net,

I padded out on to the balcony. Phew! A wall of sticky heat hit me as soon as I opened the door. It was still only about eight o' clock, but already I could feel myself beginning to sweat. I retreated hastily back inside and closed the door, savouring the coolness of the room from the air-conditioner. It made a terrible racket, whirring and banging away in the corner, but at least it provided a relatively cool haven amid the oppressive heat. Sue was still showing no signs of stirring, so I had a quick wash and pulled on a pair of shorts and T-shirt.

'Come on, aren't you getting up?' I called out. 'They'll stop serving breakfast soon.'

There was a muffled moan from under the sheet. Sue groaned: 'I don't feel too good – maybe you'd better go ahead without me. I'll get up in a minute. Could you bring me back something to drink?'

Michael was already down on the beach waiting for us. He waved eagerly when he saw me. Local traders were not allowed on to hotel property, so I headed over between the shady palm trees to speak to him.

'Look! I have found shoes for you,' he said. 'Are you ready to come? Where is your sister? She OK?'

I laughed. 'Hey, it's only just after nine! Give us time. My sister is still in the room. She's not feeling very well, but I'm sure she'll be better soon. We'll be along at ten. See you later.'

But when I got back to the room I discovered that Sue wasn't feeling at all better. She had been in and out of the toilet several times and was feeling very weak.

'It must have been that Hungarian goulash you ate last night,' I said. 'My fish was fine.' I was trying to make light of it, but I was a bit worried. She really did look awful.

'Don't worry, I'll be fine soon,' Sue said, managing a

pasty smile as she collapsed back on to the bed. 'But I guess the snorkelling's off. I'm really sorry about this. Poor Michael.' That was typical of Sue – not the slightest concern about her own health, but anxious only for the disappointment caused to others.

'You must make sure you drink plenty,' I told her. 'It's terribly hot here, and you could get dehydrated really quickly.' I sat on the edge of her bed and put my arm round her shoulders to help her sit up. There was some cold drinking water in the thermos flask provided in the room. I held the glass up to her lips, and she managed a few sips.

However, as the day wore on, I got increasingly worried about Sue. She emerged from the toilet on one occasion, her face as white as a sheet. I leapt up just in time as her eyes rolled and she crumpled on to the floor, just avoiding cracking her head on the heavy wooden luggage rack.

I realised that the most important thing was to make her drink, but that was becoming more and more difficult because she was so sleepy. By lunch-time, I knew that I needed to call the doctor.

The afternoon seemed to go on for ever. The duty doctor had promised to call round at the end of his afternoon's work, 'probably around five-ish'. As I looked at Sue, it seemed like an eternity away. What else could I do? I felt so helpless – and guilty. It was me who had asked Sue to come on this holiday. What a dreadful holiday for her to have. And what if she needed to go to hospital? I *must* get more fluids into her, I thought anxiously. Not only did she have severe diarrhoea and vomiting, but she was now also sweating profusely. I knew people could die of dehydration in a very short time, especially in a place as stiflingly hot as Mombasa.

I sat on my bed for most of the afternoon, working half-heartedly and distractedly at a small cross-stitch I had brought with me, anxiously glancing across at Sue every few moments to check that she was still breathing. It seemed that for every little bit of cross-stitch I completed, there was an even larger section that had gone wrong and needed unpicking!

'Come on, Sue. Keep drinking. *Please* try!'

Five o' clock came and went. Half-past five. Six o'clock. Where was the doctor? I wished I had told him it was an emergency, but it did not seem so bad at the time. Now I was really worried. 'Please Lord,' I prayed. 'Don't let anything happen to her. I couldn't bear it.'

At six-twenty there was a knock at the door. At last! Dumping his black attaché case on to my bed, the doctor began to prod at my sister's stomach as I explained how she had been throughout the day. 'Acute gastro-enteritis,' he announced. 'Probably something she ate. She'll be all right in a couple of days.'

'But we're due to travel back on the overnight train to Nairobi tomorrow night. Do you think she'll be fit enough by then to travel?' I did not relish the thought of an extra night in this oven with my sister so poorly.

He looked up from the form he was filling out. 'Haven't you heard? Last night's train was derailed. The trains aren't running at the moment.'

'Oh no! That's all we need,' I said.

'You might be lucky and get on a plane, if the places haven't all gone already. Why, do you need to catch your plane back to Britain?'

'Well no, not yet.' I explained the situation to him.

'My sister's going back to the UK, but my home's in Rwanda.'

'*Rwanda*!' He gasped. 'Isn't that where the president has been killed?'

'No, no,' I said. 'You're thinking of Burundi. It's next door to Rwanda – their president was killed last year.'

People often mixed up the two neighbouring countries – they were both similar size, climate and culture, and with the same ethnic divisions. The doctor was simply a little out of date with his news, I thought.

'No,' he insisted. 'It's all over the news – they've *both* been killed. Their plane crashed on Wednesday night. It's terrible what's happening over there – haven't you heard?'

I was stunned. No, I had not heard anything. My shortwave radio was sitting on the table by my bed, but I realised it was now Friday 8 April 1994 and I had not listened to it since Wednesday.

I tried hard to concentrate on his instructions about the tablets he had prescribed for Sue, but by this time my mind was in a blur. 'These are to stop the diarrhoea. She should take two now, and each time after each bout of diarrhoea. These are to stop the stomach cramps. Take one twice a day. These are antibiotics. Take two three times a day. And these are to stop her being sick. She's to take one now and another tomorrow morning. That should be enough.'

'I hope you took that in, Lesley, 'cos I certainly won't remember!' Sue mumbled weakly. She was already beginning to look a little bit brighter. 'I'll rattle with all that lot inside me!'

I could hardly wait for the doctor to go and followed him out on to the balcony, radio in hand. I was just in time for the BBC World Service seven o'clock news. Just as he'd said, Rwanda was the main headline. I could hardly believe my ears. Sure enough, the presidents of Rwanda and Burundi had both been killed in an air crash, but it sounded as though all hell had subsequently been let loose in Rwanda as a whole. The Prime Minister had been murdered, and ten Belgian United Nations troops. The names were also read out of several other government ministers who had been murdered, and the reporter was talking of thousands of civilians being slaughtered. My mind was in turmoil. What was going on? Who was doing all this killing? The newsreader described mobs of extremist Hutu militia roaming the streets of Kigali, armed with machetes and clubs; road blocks all around, and countless numbers of people were being murdered in broad daylight. The reporters were watching it all with their own eyes! What on earth had happened to the country? Why was no one stopping it?

I sat still and tried to take it all in. We had been in the country during the invasion of the RPF in October 1990. Since then, there had been numerous outbreaks of fighting around the country; Rwanda was certainly no stranger to war. This, though, sounded infinitely worse.

Sue looked up as I opened the bedroom door.

'Is it bad?' she asked.

'Oh Sue, it's *awful*.' Slumping on to the end of her bed, I buried my head in my hands as the tears streamed down my cheeks. 'What am I doing here? I should be there with Charles. What on earth is going on?'

I had no way of finding out what was going on, other than listening to the BBC. If only I could phone through to Rwanda, but out in the sticks in Gahini we had no telephones. I knew I would have to get back to Nairobi and make contact with Rwanda, but how? Sue was much too ill to travel, and the trains were not even running. We had no transport, and anyway it was a full gruelling day's drive from Mombasa to Nairobi.

A feeling of acute helplessness overwhelmed me. I wished there were someone to make decisions for me, to sort everything out. I longed to wake up and discover it had all been a horrible nightmare.

'Why, Lord?' I cried out. 'Why, when you knew how much I needed a rest? Why are these terrible things going on in Rwanda, and I'm so far from Charles? Why have you let Sue become so ill, and then left us stranded here in Mombasa, helpless? It's too much. I can't take any more.'

I did not really expect God to answer. Anyway, I had no time to listen to him. I was too busy looking after Sue, and listening in to the news on the hour, every hour. The situation just seemed to be getting worse and worse. Now they were talking of *tens* of thousands being killed. My mind reeled at the thought; I simply could not take it in.

The following morning I asked reception to phone the airport. Not surprisingly, the planes were fully booked for the next few days. There were so many other people in the same predicament as us. So now what?

Standing by the reception desk beside me was an American couple, discussing a car hire leaflet they had picked up. 'Excuse me,' I butted in. 'You're not by any chance trying to go back to Nairobi, are you?'

'Why, sure. We heard the trains aren't running, but

we've got to get back for work on Monday, so we thought we might hire a vehicle. Is that where you're heading too?'

I explained our awful situation, and within minutes we had decided to travel back together. The man seemed to be of the organising type, so gratefully I left the hiring of a car in his hands and headed back to tell Sue. We were to leave straight after lunch, stop over in Voi for the night, and should be in Nairobi by lunch-time on Sunday.

It was going to be a horrendous journey for Sue. There would not be many places to stop if she felt ill, driving the long miles through Tsavo National Park. But at least she would be able to rest properly back in the comfort of the Tear Fund flat in Nairobi. Anything had to be better than staying on in this stifling place.

Tear Fund's flat in Nairobi is a welcome sight at any time, but particularly so after a long, hot and exhausting journey. Its whitewashed walls draped with pink and red Bougainvillea looked like a palace compared to the grotty dive where we had stayed in Voi the previous night. But, most importantly of all, it was cool. There were bottles of ice-cold water in the fridge, and a pleasantly scented, clean, flush toilet. No excuse for Sue not to drink and drink, making up for the necessary self-imposed restraint on the journey.

Dumping our bags on the sitting-room floor, Sue collapsed into an armchair while I headed straight for the fax machine on the table in the corner. The paper was trailing on the floor with several messages. I picked it up to read it:

MESSAGE FOR LESLEY BILINDA
DO NOT UNDER ANY CIRCUMSTANCES ATTEMPT TO GO BACK TO RWANDA.
PLEASE PHONE TEAR FUND IMMEDIATELY.

The same message was repeated several times, together with home phone numbers of the personnel staff in London. The last message was today's, Sunday 10 April 1994, and had further information:

MESSAGE FOR LESLEY BILINDA
GAHINI PERSONNEL HAVE BEEN EVACUATED. I REPEAT, DO *NOT* ATTEMPT TO GO BACK.

My heart sank as I slumped into the chair. If my colleagues in Gahini had been evacuated, that meant things must be bad. I picked up the phone and dialled one of the numbers on the fax. Engaged. Where had I left my address book? Maybe I could try some numbers in Rwanda.

Kibungo diocese – perhaps the bishop might know whether Charles was safe. It took several attempts to get through, until at last I heard the familiar ring. No reply. I tried my sister-in-law, Diane, in Kigali. Same story. For every number I rang, either I could not get through or there was no reply. It was unbelievably frustrating. Was it the Kenyan phone system or had everyone fled from their homes? Perhaps they were hiding and dared not emerge to answer the phone. Or, much worse, I shuddered as I imagined it, perhaps they were lying dead on the floor, and the phone was just ringing, ringing, ringing.

I had one more number to ring – that of the Williams

family, a British couple and their three young boys working with the Bible Society in Kigali. This time I got through, and Chris answered. What a relief to find someone to speak to. 'What's going on, Chris? What on earth is happening?' I did not expect her to have news of Charles, but at least she could tell me something of the situation in Kigali.

They told me that they had not been able to go out since the previous Thursday – it was much too dangerous on the streets. There had been mobs in their garden; there was a road block at the top of their drive where people were being murdered; some of their neighbours had already been killed, and expatriates were being evacuated.

'So what about you,' I asked. 'Will you go or will you stay?'

Chris's voice had sounded deceptively calm as she reported these dreadful things to me, but there was no hesitation in her answer. 'Oh, we're going! Everyone who possibly can is getting out. It really is awful – much worse than 1990. We're just waiting for troops to evacuate us.'

In October 1990, when the RPF had invaded northern Rwanda from Uganda, they had advanced almost as far as Kigali. Security had been bad then, and many expatriates had left. But this time, it seemed, the situation was even more grave.

If only I'd been there, I thought to myself in despair. If only I'd been there, Charles would have been evacuated with us. Why was I so stupid as to come away without him? A wave of remorse swept through me. What help could I possibly be to him in Kenya?

Suddenly, an idea sprung into my mind. Does he not have a passport, and is he not married to me, a British citizen? Surely that should help. If the troops who're carrying out the evacuation can get to him, surely they'll take him too. That was it! If I could contact them, and let them know where to find him, he'll be all right. But I knew I would have to move quickly. The evacuation process was nearly complete, and once all the expatriates were out, it would be too late.

By nine o'clock the following morning I was in the British High Commission in Nairobi explaining my predicament to the Kenyan man on reception. Without really listening to me, he duly thrust me a form to complete and instructed me to take a seat. I looked around in despair at the room already half full of Asians and Africans, all waiting to be seen, and wrote URGENT in large black letters on my form. Every minute would count.

It worked. Within a few minutes, I was invited through to a more private office. The woman I saw was called Jill; she was warm and understanding, and listened intently as my story came tumbling out over a mug of coffee. I guessed, by the photos on her desk, that she was probably married to a Kenyan, hence the extra depth in her concern. Regretfully, there was nothing she herself could do; but she said if I waited a few minutes she would speak personally to the First Secretary (Consular).

I waited anxiously in her office, looking around me. On her desk in front of me I caught sight of a wedding invitation card with a quotation from Jeremiah, chapter 29 verse 11. 'For I know the plans I have for you,' declares the Lord, 'plans to prosper you and not to harm you, plans to give you a hope and a future.' The verse was like a cool wind blowing gently into my feverish and troubled mind. Everything around and within me seemed to be in total turmoil, yet here was a quiet reminder that my future was in God's hands. There *was* hope. It seemed to take the tension out of the moment, and for the first time in four days I sensed a drop of peace seeping into the chaos inside me.

Jill returned. 'Mr Summers will see you, if you'd like to come through now.'

True to her word, Jill had carefully reported all that I had told her, and the First Secretary had felt it was a case worth following up. That in itself was encouraging. However, it soon became clear that this would not be an easy task. There was no British Ambassador in Rwanda. We tried to telephone the British consul, but learned that he had already left with the other expatriates, so there was no British representative at all left in Rwanda.

'The consul is due to fly in to Nairobi later this afternoon, so we'll see if he has any news. Perhaps your husband will be on the plane.'

He did not seem to have fully grasped the situation.

'That's impossible,' I insisted. 'How on earth could he get to the airport? He doesn't have transport, and no one would know to go and pick him up. He *cannot* get out unless someone goes to collect him. *Please* try to get the Belgian soldiers to go and pick him up too.'

In the weeks prior to the outbreak of the war, we had had visits in Gahini from both French and Belgian military. They were compiling lists of all expatriates in the country and explaining procedures in the event of an evacuation. Charles's name was on those lists; surely they must be expecting to evacuate him too?

But the problem was that they would have to know where to find him. Slowly and clearly, I described how to locate the house where he was staying while Mr

Summers carefully wrote down the details. He admitted that he did not hold out much hope of anyone helping, but was certainly willing to try every possible avenue. It would just be a question of some phone calls . . .

Just some phone calls. In Kenya, of course, that is no simple matter. I sat for what seemed like hours, waiting with increasing frustration as the telephone system did its worst. The British Embassy in Uganda; five numbers for the Belgian Embassy in Kigali; the Foreign Office in London. We were lucky if one attempt in every ten actually made a connection.

There seemed to be nothing to be gained by my sitting there waiting. This was clearly going to take some time, so I felt that perhaps I should pursue some other options in the meantime. Mr Summers suggested that I speak with the representatives at the Belgian Embassy in Nairobi. Within fifteen minutes, I was there.

'List? What list of British citizens? We know nothing about it. We are not responsible for the evacuation of the British. Why don't you contact your Embassy in Kigali?'

'But we don't have an Embassy in Kigali! That's the point. That's why I've come to speak to you!' The heavily made-up Belgian woman in reception was right in saying she knew nothing about it. If she did not even know that there was no British Embassy in Kigali, there was not much hope.

'There's a plane coming in from Kigali in a few minutes. Perhaps your husband will be arriving on that,' she added. It was obvious that this woman was not in the slightest bit interested in me.

'I told you, that's out of the question. There's no way

he could possibly get to the airport. The only way is if he is collected from . . .'

'Go to your Embassy here in Nairobi then,' she responded curtly. 'They should help you. Now who's next please?'

'But I've just come from there,' I protested, rapidly losing my patience. 'They suggested I come to see *you*!'

A distraught young Belgian girl was standing at the reception desk beside me. She wanted news of a friend who had been sightseeing in Rwanda, but her enquiries elicited the same frosty, unhelpful response as mine had.

This exercise was obviously pointless; I was a nobody as far as they were concerned. Perhaps the British High Commission was my best hope after all. At least the First Secretary would have some authority, and be able to make direct contact with those with influence. If he could get through to them on the phone, that is.

Over the next two days the efforts continued. Tear Fund was also making contact with the Foreign Office in London; I refused to lose hope as long as there was still some avenue we had not tried. On Tuesday afternoon I went back to see Mr Summers.

'I'm afraid, Lesley, we've tried everything we possibly can. It would be impossible for troops to go to look for your husband. It is an extremely delicate situation politically, and if it were known that a Rwandan were being singled out for evacuation, it could jeopardise the whole evacuation procedure. I'm terribly sorry not to be of any more help to you, but there really is nothing more we can do. Do you understand that?'

I understood only too well. I suppose I had not really expected that they would be able to help, but I had to try everything possible. We shook hands, and I tried to

thank him for all his help, although I could barely
speak.

I made my way slowly back to the flat. Everything
looked very black indeed. The operation to evacuate
expatriates was now almost complete, and Charles was
stranded in his own country, an educated Tutsi, a
prime target. How could he possibly survive? Never in
my life had I felt so desperately low. The mad rushing
around, endless telephone calls, pleadings and per-
suadings, feeling constantly that time was rapidly running out. It was all over. Now there was nothing I
could do.

I thought again about trying to get back into Rwanda
to look for him, but how would I begin? For a start, I
would have no transport, and even if I did, it would be
suicide to travel alone with road blocks every few
hundred yards on all roads. It was now known that the
president's plane had been shot down, although no one
knew who was responsible. Perhaps it was shot by
extremist elements of the Hutu Presidential Guard,
angry that the president had signed an agreement to
share power with the opposition parties (including the
mainly Tutsi RPF) and therefore afraid that they would
lose their own power. Or perhaps it was shot by the
RPF as a prelude to beginning the war? No one seemed
to know.

The mainly Hutu extremist militia, however,
together with elements of the Rwandan army, were
responsible for the majority of the ongoing killings.
Their targets were initially both Hutu and Tutsi, those
known for their moderate political views and therefore
seen as a threat to the maintenance of power by the
extremists. But soon all Tutsi were branded as RPF
accomplices and singled out for killing – thousands

upon thousands of them every day. The RPF were heading south from their positions in the north of Rwanda, but they could do little to stop the mass slaughter.

As far as the militia were concerned, being married to a Tutsi was considered the same as being a Tutsi, so if I attempted to travel to Rwanda I would probably not make it past the first road block. In one of my phone calls home I had learned of the murder of two friends of ours. He was a Tutsi married to a Belgian woman; the colour of her skin had offered her no protection. Anyway, if Charles were hiding, my searching would only draw attention to him, and if he had already fled, where would I go to look for him?

No, there was nothing to be gained by going back. And there was absolutely nothing more I could do but wait. For how long, though?

Somehow I made it back to the flat. I went straight to my room and flung myself on to my bed. 'Oh Lord, this is unbearable. What can I do?' I sobbed into my pillow, and tried to relate to Sue the fruitless results of my frantic activity. 'Is there nothing else we can do? We can't just sit here while thousands are being hacked up every day.'

It was a terrible, terrible feeling. The situation was totally out of our hands. We were completely helpless. Or were we?

The words from the end of Psalm 20 suddenly came vividly to mind: 'Some trust in chariots and some in horses, but we trust in the name of the Lord our God. They are brought to their knees and fall, but we rise up and stand firm' (Psalm 20:7–8). What were the modern-day 'chariots' and 'horses' if not the Belgian army and the United Nations troops carrying out the evacuation? And if they cannot do anything, does that mean all is lost? Surely not. Like a flash from heaven, it felt as if the Lord was clearly reminding me that he has no need of human intervention. Could I not trust *him* to do what others had found impossible?

'I'm so slow!' I chided myself. 'Why do I always turn to God as a last resort? Pray! Of course! We must pray for Charles. Surely God can keep him safe in the midst of that awful situation even if troops can't do anything.'

Sue was of the same mind entirely, and so together we began to pray. In fact, we prayed at every possible moment. Charles was always on my mind, and so I constantly brought him before the Lord.

But still the massacres continued in Rwanda, and I began to wonder, 'Why should I pray for Charles's safety, when it seems so many are being slaughtered? Is that not selfish? Why should God be any more likely to answer my prayer, when presumably there are thousands praying for protection and peace, and yet still the killing goes on? Who was I to think that he would answer me?'

Questions such as these were there, but so were the passages of encouragement from the Bible: 'If two of you on earth agree about anything you ask for, it will be done for you by my Father in Heaven' (Matthew 18:19), 'But when he asks, he must believe and not doubt' (James 1:6), 'Now faith is being sure of what we hope for and certain of what we do not see' (Hebrews 11:1) and many others.

It seemed to Sue and me that God was encouraging us to persevere, and not to give up. Maybe we did not have faith to pray that God would end the suffering in Rwanda, but we were to have faith to pray for this one particular person.

*

My British colleagues from Gahini had left Rwanda by road, crossing over into Tanzania. Apparently there had been some killing in the first few days, and Rob's life had been threatened. This news, though, was relayed to me from London, and there were no details of who was involved. Would it be people I knew? I thought about my friends back there and shivered at the thought of them caught up helplessly in these terrible events. Some of the Gahini expatriates had opted to stay in Tanzania, but others were hoping to continue their journey and were due to arrive in Nairobi the following day.

Wilson Airport in Nairobi was used mainly for small planes, and seemed to have remarkably lax security procedures. I was already on the tarmac and running towards the plane by the time the first passengers began to file down the steps. There were hugs all around, and we headed towards the small customs building.

I wanted to ask immediately about those who had been killed, but I was afraid to. I felt sure there would be someone I knew well. Everyone was speaking at once, telling me all that had happened.

There was no news of Charles.

We reached the passport control and formed a queue. I found myself standing at the end with two of the girls who were relatively recent arrivals in Gahini. The others were fumbling for their passports.

Eventually I plucked up the courage to ask, 'Do you know who it was who was killed?'

They looked at each other for a moment without replying. I knew immediately by their hesitation that my fears were realised.

'Are you sure you really want to know?' asked one of them gently.

'Just tell me,' I said impatiently, 'I've got to know sooner or later.'

There was a moment's hesitation, and then one of the girls said, 'Well, there were not many by the time we left, and most of them we didn't know – they weren't hospital staff. But . . .' she fumbled for words. 'But they killed Anatolie. Oh Lesley, I'm so sorry. Apparently they came to her house to look for her husband, and he wasn't there, so they killed her instead. They macheted her little girl too, quite badly, but she survived.'

Anatolie! They've killed Anatolie? Why? What had she ever done to anyone? My head was reeling. Anatolie, my right-hand woman all the time I had been in Rwanda. My friend, the best colleague anyone could ever ask for. Dead? *Murdered*? It can't be. But she devoted herself to that community. Is this the reward she gets now?

Extreme anger burned inside me. How *dare* anyone take the life of such a gracious, selfless, innocent woman? And Liliose, her daughter. She was only *three*! As if there had not been enough tragedy in that little girl's life, seeing her six-year-old sister die suddenly of malaria only two months ago. And now this. Her mother murdered, and she attacked with machetes.

'Do you know who did it?' I asked quietly.

'I don't think they know exactly, but it's said that Habakkuk's sons were among the killers.'

That did not surprise me, but it disgusted me none the less. This local churchman was not well liked in many circles, and his sons had been suspected of involvement in sinister business on several occasions in the past, but no one had been able to pin them down.

What kind of madness had overtaken the country that caused people to murder one another in cold blood? I just could not begin to imagine, let alone understand. My mind was in a blur. It was as if I was not living in reality. Somewhere I had to function – to get these people through customs, into the car, back to the flat, eat lunch. Life had to carry on, but it had left me behind somewhere.

There was plenty to keep me occupied over the next few days. Endless phone calls – each one of which took at least six tries before getting through; people to be collected from the airport and accommodation to be arranged; trips into town to the British High Commission. And every day trying in vain, time after time, to make contact with Rwanda.

As other British colleagues came out of Rwanda, I was able to get more information. But still nothing about Charles. They told me again how our Tutsi friend and his Belgian wife had both been killed in Kigali, together with his elderly father, a very special friend of ours from Gahini.

My head was full of endless questions. Perhaps if I had been in Rwanda when the troubles broke out I would have been killed too, as the wife of a Tutsi? Or would we have both been able to get out safely? The Gahini folk had travelled by road to Tanzania, past several road blocks. These road blocks were set up with the express purpose of checking the identity of every single traveller, and weeding out the Tutsis. If Charles had been with us in the car, I knew that it was quite possible that the mobs at the road blocks would have dragged him from the car and slaughtered him before my very eyes.

I could not bear to think of it. Perhaps it was just as
well I was not there. Imagine having to make a decision
to leave him there, knowing he would probably be
killed if he tried to escape with us? Or if I decided to
stay on with him, we might both have been killed. As
it was, without a white woman in tow to draw attention
to him, he just might have a better chance of survival.

God had overruled in all this, and taken such
decisions out of my hands. The only question now was
when would I get news of him? Or when would I be
able to get back into Rwanda to look for him? I had
decided to stay on in Nairobi so as to be able to travel
straight back in as soon as the situation had sufficiently
calmed down. Yet it was becoming clear from the news
and from those still coming out that we would have to
wait a long time for normality to be restored. Things
were still getting worse with every passing day.

By this time, I was completely exhausted. I was not
sleeping well, I had no appetite, and I had been rushing
around non-stop for the past week. The flat was always
full of people, noise and activity. And all this on top of
the accumulated stress of the past months – the very
reason I had come to Kenya for a holiday in the first
place.

Slowly, it dawned on me that there was nothing to
be gained from staying on in Nairobi. When news
about Charles eventually came through, it would be as
easy to jump on a plane from London as from Nairobi.
For now I had to trust him to the Lord. We were
praying with faith that God would be keeping him safe,
providing for him, strengthening him wherever he was.
What happened to him was totally out of my control,
yet totally in God's control.

It was a profound lesson to me of recognising my own severe limitations and helplessness, and yet knowing that I was a child of the very Creator of the universe, to whom nothing is impossible.

So on 17 April 1994, Sue and I flew back to the UK together. The long, long wait in the darkness had begun.

6

Agony and Uncertainty in the UK

I set the plate of steaming hot food on the table in front of me, and paused to thank God for it. But no words came. And I could not even bring myself to eat it. How could I tuck in to a nutritious, fresh and delicious meal when those I loved were starving, sick and terrified? I sunk my head into my hands and wept.

Images and memories flashed through my mind, all mixed up together. Yes, I was grateful for my safety, a home and food. Yet if I could have packed it all up and sent it out to my friends in Rwanda, I would gladly have done so. How could I eat while they had nothing?

I must have sat for about half an hour, struggling to accept my lot, before putting a bite of now cold food into my mouth. A little bit of common sense told me I had to eat. I was still losing weight, despite having plenty of healthy food around.

It was the same story day after day. Materially I had everything around me I could want, yet there was a heaviness in the pit of my stomach, like a lump of lead dragging me down and keeping me from eating.

When we arrived in London, Sue caught a train straight back to Edinburgh to her family. But I could not yet face reunions with family and friends, so had opted to stay on in London for a short while. Sue Mills, Tear Fund's personnel manager for Africa, had promised to arrange accommodation for me. She could not have been kinder. Vacating her own flat for as long as I wanted to stay there, she had stocked up the cupboards, the fridge and the fruit bowl with essentials as well as luxuries. I felt thoroughly spoiled by her love and thoughtfulness.

For the next few weeks I had a place of my own, a haven of peace, after the chaos, confusion and busyness of Nairobi. And I so needed it. Most of the time I just wanted to be alone. The frantic rushing around, making arrangements, being constantly surrounded by people, had not allowed me the space to begin to come to terms with the situation. I needed to stop all the frantic activity and to try to face up to what was happening.

Yet that was an incredibly painful thing to do. On the one hand, the slaughter in Rwanda continued unabated; and on the other hand, somehow I continued to believe that Charles would be safe, that God was looking after him.

I began to keep a diary. 'Impression without expression leads to depression' the psychiatrist had said to me when I had a routine debriefing session a few days after my return. I found it difficult to express myself by talking to people because there were so many thoughts racing through my mind one after the other; I did not even know where to begin. But I could try to write.

Thus my days were filled with many hours of reflection and writing in my diary, and punctuated with regular news bulletins on the radio and television. The news only got worse, though, and left me feeling even more despondent. The following are some of the entries in my diary:

Friday, 22 April
NATO is increasing its offensive against the Serbs in Bosnia because of the 'atrocities' being committed there, but the UN is pulling out of Rwanda!!!! The number of people *already* killed in Rwanda is thought to be about twice the population of the whole of Gorazde!! Is that not an atrocity which is still going on? All the UN is doing in Rwanda is being a presence – but their presence is protecting thousands of people. Why can they not stay? It makes me sick. Just because Bosnia is white and Rwanda is black . . .

On 26 April, for once Rwanda was not the first item on the news. A miracle was happening in South Africa. For the first time ever in its history, it had gone to the polls. I watched the calm and orderly queues of thousands upon thousands of people, standing patiently in the hot sun, waiting their turn to vote. I watched Bishop Desmond Tutu, unable to hide his excitement, wave his hands triumphantly in the air as he dropped his vote in the box, crying out 'Yipeeee' to the delighted journalists, the nation and the world. Their years of injustice, oppression and apartheid had at last come to an end. I wept for joy with them.

But then in stark contrast, further up the same continent, came more news of carnage and horror in Rwanda; more pictures of burned-out homes, of decimated, blood-splattered bodies strewn on the ground; more reports of killings and torture beyond description. And the tears flowed yet again:

Saturday, 30 April
... Further reports today and yesterday speak of between a quarter and three-quarters of a million Rwandans who fled across to Tanzania within twenty-four hours – the largest and fastest exodus the UN has ever known. Then today the BBC suggests that up to 500,000 people may have been slaughtered in the last three weeks. That's 6 per cent of the whole population. How can anyone grieve for that number of people all at once?

Boutros Boutros Ghali has asked the UN Security Council to send troops to end the massacre – and they responded by calling for an arms embargo! It's unbelievable! Just what difference is that going to make to the militia massacres of civilians? Who's going to take their machetes out of their hands, or ban the sale of nails for making clubs?

Monday, 2 May
... Switched on the radio for the news, and I hear Rwanda being described as the biggest human catastrophe the world has known since Cambodia in the seventies, with three-quarters of a million people either already dead or facing imminent death through slaughter or starvation. I listen again in disbelief. I hear the word 'Rwanda' and think, 'There must be some mistake. Surely they mean somewhere else, not the tiny unknown little country which had become my homeland. It can't be true.'

But it is. The nightmare is reality. And as I sit in my comfy armchair sipping tea and eating a toasted crumpet and honey, I'm numbed again by the injustice and the incomprehensibility of the world and by the strong evil control Satan has on people, inciting them to such unbelievable wickedness. When will it all end? Surely all hell has been unleashed on Rwanda? How else can such rampant evil be described? Why has the influence of a few godly people not had any staying power? Why is God allowing such destruction in one little country while the rest of the world looks on, powerless – or in some cases with the power to intervene, but no will?

There have now been four weeks of unrelenting slaughter. When will it all end? Who will be left? Only *Interahamwe* [the militia] and the RPF? I want some answers and explanations, but I will never have them. There are none.

On Wednesday, 4 May, there was a long item on each news bulletin showing scenes from Gahini, as well as our local Catholic church at Rukara. All around and inside the church were hundreds of bloody corpses strewn on the ground, slumped between the benches. I just sat stunned, numbed yet again by the horror of it all. Each time I heard or saw something new, I thought it must be the worst thing ever, but there was always worse to come, and each time it numbed me afresh.

This was darkness indeed. Where was God now? I picked up my pen and began to write:

Where are you, Lord?
  as bloated bodies float face down in the river;
  as thousands wander aimlessly in a strange land,
  feet blistered, shivering with the cold,
  separated from loved ones by bereavement,
  hungry, lonely, exhausted,
  aimless and helpless,

drinking from the poisoned waters of the Kagera
– poisoned with rotting, severed limbs and bodies?

Where are you, Lord?
   as children are massacred in YOUR house,
   where they thought you would protect them;
   as the sick and wounded,
   'lucky' enough to survive the first attempt,
   are brutally slaughtered on their hospital beds?

Where are you, Lord?
   as the sleek, fat politicians of the West
   play games with precious life created by you,
   pour resources into Bosnia but
   pull out the tiny glimmer of hope in Rwanda;
   as they procrastinate over bureaucracy
   while 5,000 innocent lives are lost each day?

Where are you, Lord?

I had no answers. Not one. This was far, far beyond
anything I had ever faced before.

The tragedies were happening on two levels for me:
the personal and intimate agony of being separated
from Charles and not knowing what was happening to
him; and the wider horror of the whole of Rwanda with
its vast implications. I could not begin to grasp either
of them.

Yet sometimes in the midst of my deepest agonies I
sensed a deep and very real sense of peace. Not a peace
from outward circumstances; not a peace from material
security or happiness. Outwardly, there was nothing
whatsoever in my life that should allow me to feel
any peace at all. This was a peace that was as incomprehensible as the situation itself. It was like being in the
tiny pinpoint of calm at the centre of a massive whirl-

wind, when all around the wind is whipping up disaster upon disaster. On Sunday, 24 April, I wrote the following:

> . . . I have been stripped in one fell swoop of so much that made up my life – my husband, my home, my job, some of my dear friends – and faced with a *very* uncertain and totally unknown future. That's pretty mega all at once.
>
> But at the bottom of it all, God is still there. I *know* he is still in control, and that he *will* bring good out of all this. I've lost everything which gave me identity and value and have been thrown on to God totally. I'm not enjoying the experience. Far from it. It's inexpressibly painful. But in a way it's a mysterious and awesome privilege . . .
>
> I have no need to pretend, to put on a front, to prove myself. I couldn't anyway. I'm just empty, totally helpless, and at rock bottom. BUT, I'm full of peace! God is a solid rock. I can't fall any farther. The verses I read this morning are so true:
>
> 'Underneath are the everlasting arms' (Deuteronomy 33:27). 'The Lord delights in the way of the man whose steps he has made firm; though he stumble, he will not fall, for the Lord upholds him with his hand' (Psalm 37:23–4).

It was a calm I could not understand or begin to explain, but it was as real to me as was the holocaust in Rwanda. I had been a Christian for nearly twenty years. I had known in my head that God was real, that he was my heavenly Father, and I his child, but my life had been relatively smooth and straightforward. I had never really had to put my faith to the test.

Now, for the first time in my life, I was coming face

to face with the practical outworking of what I had known theoretically for so many years, and I found it to be overwhelmingly true. There was no way I could work up such an inexplicable peace by my own efforts. I was totally exhausted; finished. And yet I *knew* God my Father was there with me, loving me, holding me, comforting me. I knew now from the bottom of my heart, not just in my head, that he *is* real and that his promises are true.

This knowing did not take away the questions, though, or the confusion about why all this had happened. I continued to pray for Charles's safety and protection, day in, day out. I knew God was all powerful and could easily look after him, however awful the circumstances around him, but the more I watched atrocity after atrocity on the television, the more I began to wonder why it was that some individuals would be protected while others would be killed. Why did I think that God should care for Charles, when people like Anatolie, or Eustace Kajuga, another dear friend of ours, had been killed? Yet I still felt it was right to pray earnestly for him.

I read again the story in Matthew's Gospel of Peter walking on the water. As soon as Peter took his eyes off Jesus and looked at the wind and the waves around him, he began to sink and called out, 'Lord, save me'. And immediately Jesus reached out his hand and caught him, saying, 'You of little faith. Why did you doubt?' It seemed to me that I was to keep my eyes fixed on Jesus and his ability to save Charles, and not to be overwhelmed by the horrors in Rwanda.

It was a very strange experience to be so totally out of control of almost every aspect of my life, and yet at the same time not to need to be in control:

Monday, 25 April

. . . In our ordered lives we're so used to knowing and being in control. Sometimes we have decisions to make about our future – career move, marriage, moving house etc. But it's usually one thing at a time, and we remain secure in one area until it becomes clear the next direction we should move to. But I have NOTHING! Everything has gone in one fell swoop, and I don't know anything about the future! That's very weird. So much is an unknown quantity – 'what if . . . ? what if . . . ?' It's all completely out of my hands. But I guess that's good.

As I read through sections of the Bible each day, I often found the passages spoke directly into my thinking at the time. That day I read:

> Trust in the Lord with all your heart
>   and lean not on your own understanding;
> in all your ways acknowledge him,
>   and he will make your paths straight
> (Proverbs 3:5–6).

and:

> Trust in the Lord and do good;
>   dwell in the land and enjoy safe pasture.
> Delight yourself in the Lord
>   and he will give you the desires of your heart.
> Commit your way to the Lord . . .
> Be still before the Lord
>   and wait patiently for him (Psalm 37:3–7).

That day's entry in my diary continued:

I'm *having* to learn a dependency on God which I'd never begin to know if everything was clear cut and dried. And even at such a depth and intensity of helplessness maybe I could cope for a few days if the end were in sight. But with no end in sight, and the unknown stretching out indefinitely before me, I can only cling to him and commit myself and all my uncertainties into his hands again and again and again. Once isn't enough. I may have come to a point of acceptance now, but I'll have to weep and wrestle with it many times to come, I'm sure.

Yet it was one thing to sit in the safety and peace of Sue's flat wrestling with all these big issues. It would be quite another to go out and face the world again, and particularly to go back to Rwanda. That thought, though, was never far away.

Sue and the other staff at Tear Fund had been extremely understanding and supportive of me, as had been the very few friends that I felt I could face during these three traumatic weeks. Yet I knew that I could not hide from the world for ever. Eventually I would have to mix again with those who were indifferent to the plight of Rwanda, and who were not in the least bit interested in my situation. Those whose families, jobs and homes were secure and intact, for whom life was pleasant and comfortable. But my world had fallen apart, so how could I face them? And anyway, *should* I be facing them? Should I not be heading back out to Rwanda, or to that vast, chaotic refugee camp in Tanzania?

By the end of April 1994 there were reported to be around half a million Rwandan refugees who had fled to Tanzania. The aid agencies were completely over-

whelmed. With my nursing skills and some knowledge
of the language and customs, I felt I ought to be able to
be of some use. Under normal circumstances I knew I
could have helped, but I was reluctantly having to
realise that for the time being I could not cope with the
emotional trauma involved.

Clearly it was not right to go back to Rwanda yet,
but I could not sit around in Sue Mills's flat for ever. In
the end I decided to go back to Scotland, and arranged
to stay in Edinburgh with my sister Sue, her husband
and five children. Because Sue had been in Kenya with
me when it all broke out, she of all people would come
nearest to understanding something of my agonies.

I caught the train to Scotland on 7 May. It was a
bright and crisp late spring day, and I travelled with
my diary on my lap:

> Just looking out of the window at the beautiful
> Scottish coast – blue sea, shady cliffs with soft
> green young crops along the tops, bright yellow
> gorse and crispy clouds in the blue sky. It is
> beautiful. But a far cry from these muddy, smoky
> Tanzanian plains, swarming with shivering,
> lonely, shattered lives, as far as the eye can see. A
> far cry from the rotting bodies scattered around
> Rukara church. Is this the same world? My heart
> so longs to be there, yet I know I couldn't cope . . .

The busy family atmosphere at Sue's home was a
sharp contrast to my life as a hermit in London, but it
was good to be part of this normality. Slowly I began
to be able to meet other people and to chat about things
other than Rwanda.

But still the carnage continued, and again and again
I would be overwhelmed by the news coming out. The

scale of this horror is just absolutely unbelievable,' I
wrote on 14 May. 'I *still* – nearly six weeks into the
killing – read a newspaper article and sit numbed and
feeling sick. People are now saying that there are no
Tutsis left to kill – 80,000 or so have fled, and a few
thousand more in the camps. Where are the rest out of
1.5 million? I just can't conceive of that number of
people having been killed.'

Of my British colleagues who had fled Gahini, some
had decided to stay on in Tanzania, joining friends just
over the border at Murgwanza, a small Anglican
mission similar to Gahini. They were therefore on the
spot when the hundreds of thousands of refugees
crossed into Tanzania at the end of April.

Rob, our doctor from Gahini, found himself directly
involved. Remarkably, among the quarter of a million
people there, he met up with some of the staff from the
Gahini Hospital, and he sent us news of them. Grace
was also there, and Etienne. What wonderful news! But
there was no mention of Emeralde and the children, or
Granny, or all the rest of the family. What had happened to them? Had they stayed behind? Had they all
been killed? Straight away I sat down and wrote to
them.

There was still no news of Charles – not that I really
expected any. I did not think that he would have fled
to Tanzania, but imagined he would probably be in
hiding somewhere, unable to come out into the open,
and far less be able to find some way of contacting me.
The telephones were not working anyway, and there
was almost no movement in and out of the country,
except for the media. By this time, I was prepared for a
long wait before receiving any news.

However, the first news was not long in coming, and

on Thursday, 19 May, a phone call brought me some information. Charles had allegedly been in Butare, in south-west Rwanda, at the home of a friend and his wife, and they had all been killed. It was only a rumour, not confirmed, and I did not know its source. I knew that rumours were rife in these situations, and the chances were it was probably not true. None the less, it threw me completely.

Up until then I had believed that God was looking after Charles; I had not really faced the possibility that he might be killed. Therefore this news was shattering. Had my faith been misplaced, or should I ignore the rumour and continue to pray regardless? 'No, I don't think it's right to give up hope,' I wrote. 'From a purely practical point of view, unless his death were to be confirmed, there's no way I could live my life now assuming he had been killed, because he may turn up any day. I will go on believing he's still alive and praying for him – for years if need be . . .'

Yet my emotions could not respond as my reason could. In my heart I feared the rumour was true, and wrote as follows in my diary:

Why, oh why? Why did Charles have to die? Why, when so many people are praying for him? Again this morning as I thought about it, it just broke me and I wept and wept. I began to read of the UN proposition to go back into Rwanda, and just thought 'Why bother? What's the point now?' I feel the whole bottom of my world has dropped out again. Empty, hopeless, flat. The future seems so bleak. What's the point of going on? How can there be *so* much pain, sadness and loss in such a short time? Why?

But in pouring it all out, I do sense a slight lifting of the darkness – that somehow God will enable me to carry on in this. Perhaps mine is the greater privilege – knowing (although I'm not yet sure), that Charles is in heaven at rest and peace, and being carried through all this grief and loss in God's own hands. Perhaps having smooth solutions and all prayers answered leads to a shallower experience of God and of life.

This is *so* hard. But there is no way to put the clocks back or to take away my pain. And the only way I can make anything out of this hell, or even just keep going from day to day, is by God's strength alone.

Moving to Edinburgh brought new challenges. By now the media had heard about my situation and were eager to find out more. My diary began to fill up with speaking engagements around the country – at various groups and churches. I wanted so much to tell people about the plight of Rwanda to encourage prayer, financial support of the refugees and political awareness.

Yet this work was not without personal cost. I was still in a state of grief and uncertainty, which in itself was exhausting. But on top of that was the travelling, preparing talks, and sharing publicly my own personal trauma while still living through it. Each time I prepared to speak at a meeting, I wondered how I would ever manage to get through to the end without breaking down. But each time I put myself into Jesus' hands and left it all with him – and amazingly, out of my brokenness and helplessness, he seemed to bring encouragement and challenge to other people.

In mid-June I received my first letters from Benaco refugee camp in Tanzania. One was written in Etienne's handwriting so I quickly turned to the last page and found that it was signed, 'Etienne, Emeralde and the children'. So they were alive – not just Etienne, but Emeralde and the children too! 'Oh thank you, Lord!' I exclaimed, my hands trembling as I began to read. 'To our dear child Lesley, whom we miss very much, greetings. Are you at peace with God? How are your parents and all the family?' began the letter from Etienne and Emeralde. 'We're OK. We are refugees at present in Tanzania in a place called Benaco which is about 20 km from Rusumo [on the Rwanda/Tanzania border]. We praise God for the way he brought us here and for all his grace towards us.'

Without a hint of anger or bitterness towards God for what had happened to them, they went on to tell me of the family members who were with them, and of those who had stayed behind or were missing. They now had seven children, six of whom had fled with them, together with Granny and her other nine grand-children. They had travelled many days and nights, fleeing south towards the border with Tanzania. The letter continued:

> We brought the cows part of the way, but it became too difficult for us. When we got to Kibungo there was a lot of shooting, so we decided to flee with the children and leave the cows in Kibungo. Your cow was a really nice one [the bride-price cow which they had received at our wedding]. We were very sad not to be able to continue with them, but we praise God that we are alive and trust him that he will provide others for us.

I could hardly believe what I was reading! Their concern was for me, in case I should be sad that they had to leave 'my' cow behind! If only I could have told them of my exuberant joy to hear they were still alive. Who cared about the cow! Their account went on:

We praise him even more that since we arrived here in Tanzania he has continued to show us his love and his promises that he will be with us and those who trust him wherever they are. Before too long we were thrilled to find work with the Red Cross here in Tanzania. There are many people here with whom we were working in Gahini Hospital. In a way, it's as if we were at home . . .

Our situation is that we are in a little hut built with plastic sheeting. We are fine except Ezekiel [their two-year-old son] has been very ill because there is no milk or food he is used to here. The older children have got used to the hard corn and beans . . .

Grace's letter described the terror they had felt when the killing began and they had to flee: 'God kept us in a very real way. Each day I was expecting to die – but we didn't . . . There were masses of road blocks on the road. They called us rebels and wanted to kill us. They asked us for money. We gave it to them until there was none left. They killed an awful lot of people. Others they took their cars from them, or their nice clothes and other things . . .' I ached for her as I read of the conditions she lived in:

Do you remember the word 'plastic bag'? That is what we live in. Do you remember those sacks which had sugar in them? That is our door. We lie

down here like cows. Do you remember the house
for the cows at Etienne's? These cows had a really
nice house. We have really bad conditions to sleep
in . . . The food has caused us so many problems. I
tell you the truth, if you saw me you wouldn't
recognise me. I've lost an awful lot of weight and
turned really black . . .

She went on to describe the extortionate prices of
food on the black market, the intense heat, the illnesses
and news of others from Gahini: 'I've told you so much
news – the reason why is that my heart is broken and I
cry so much.' And yet in the midst of such hardship
and pain she still managed to be positive:

But there is good news too. We brought our Bibles
and hymn books and we meet together for prayer
on Tuesdays, Fridays and Sundays. We have
realised that this is a school we are in, in order that
we learn to fear God . . . Sitting on the ground we
have not one thing to boast of – both the 'important' people and the least important, we are all on
the same low level. We have no riches left. We
have learned that the things of this world are
worth nothing (Ecclesiastes 3:1–4).

I read, translated, and re-read their letters again and
again. I was deeply challenged and humbled by their
honesty and their faith. To be thrown into the most dire
of all circumstances imaginable – and yet to be able to
praise God in the midst of it! What unmistakable
evidence of a deep and mature faith. What a testimony
to the power of Jesus Christ to sustain and strengthen
in the midst of the horrors. And what a privilege to be
able to share in their experiences. I often spoke of these

dear people and quoted from their letters in my own letters, and as I travelled around the country speaking to churches.

Saturday, 2 July, marked eighteen months since Charles and I had got married, and on that day came a second rumour as to Charles's fate. Subsequent to the first rumour, I had learned that of the couple he was allegedly with, the husband was in fact killed alone in his office, and the wife was now in Burundi. So what had been reported to me had obviously not been true. Was this second rumour any more likely to be true?

Once again, Charles was said to have been in Butare, but this time he was apparently at the guest house of the Anglican diocese. I was told that the only two guests had been taken from there at night-time by the *Interahamwe*. As they had not been seen again, the assumption was that they had been killed. 'An understandable assumption,' I wrote, ' – only I don't share it. It's not conclusive evidence *at all*. No. I'm sure he's alive somewhere, and I'll pray on . . .'

Yet it was becoming increasingly difficult to pray on for Charles's protection. As well as the struggles in my own heart, my dilemma was to know what to say as I continued to speak to the media and to churches and meetings around the country. I had made a public stance, affirming my trust in God to look after Charles. So should I continue with this, despite the rumours? Or should I admit that I might have been wrong and that all this time he had been in heaven?

Waiting without knowing was incredibly difficult. At times I felt I did not need to know, that it was all in the Lord's hands, not mine. But at other times the agony of my own personal situation pierced me right in the centre of my heart, and I would be overwhelmed by frustration and grief. 'I want to know Lord,' I would cry out, lying prostrate on the floor, hammering my fists into the carpet. 'Why won't you tell me? Is he alive or is he dead? I can't bear this waiting any longer.'

There was, of course, never the answer I wanted; but there was a gentle, gracious reminder from God. My reading one such day was Psalm 27. I desperately wanted an answer, and read through the Psalm frustrated that there did not seem to be anything directly relevant. Until, that is, I reached the last verse:

> Wait for the Lord;
> be strong and take heart
> and wait for the Lord (Psalm 27:14).

And once again, for a while at least, a sense of peace filled my heart, replacing the turmoil and uncertainty. Yet it was always like being on an emotional roller-coaster – the highs and the lows – clinging on just to keep going.

I began to think a lot more over these summer weeks about the possibility of going back to Rwanda. Since the RPF had taken over the country in July there was now some measure of stability, and I desperately wanted to try to find out news of Charles for myself. There were other Rwandans I had heard of who had initially been rumoured dead, but had since turned up alive. That continued to give me hope that perhaps Charles too might be safe. Rumours were notoriously unreliable; I needed to find out the truth for myself.

Tear Fund, who had continued to support me in every respect, once again came up with a generous and thoughtful response to my suggestion of going back on a visit. They agreed that I needed to go back, but that it would be too tough to go alone. How would I feel, they asked, about travelling with Jennifer Loughlin, the Director of Personnel? In her professional capacity, Jennifer was more than capable of being the wise support I would need; and personally, although I did not know her well, I sensed that we would get on well.

As far as timing was concerned, the suggestion was to leave towards the end of September. But it seemed such a long way off. Having made the decision to go, I was itching to get moving as soon as possible. At the same time, though, I was increasingly nervous at the prospect of returning. It was relatively painless to stand up in a meeting and encourage people to pray for a spirit of forgiveness and reconciliation among Rwandans. But how would I feel if faced with those who had killed Anatolie, or who may have killed Charles?

I watched on television some of those who were said to be responsible for the genocide, denying that they had done anything wrong, justifying their actions. It made my blood boil. How could I go back and live among such people? I knew I had nothing in me that would enable me to forgive them, yet it was what I must do. The Bible's teaching on forgiveness and Jesus' example were crystal clear.

Being back in Rwanda would also mean constant reminders of Charles. We had spent only a short time in the UK together, so very little of my life here was associated with him. Yet in Rwanda he was a very large part of my life; so many people, places and situations were intimately connected with him. It would be so hard to go back, and for him not to be there.

Indeed there would be so much about the country that would have changed. How would I cope? An English missionary friend of mine had recently gone back on a visit, and told me of the intense sadness she had felt on leaving the country. It was no longer the Rwanda she knew. Before the war everyone had spoken the same language, Kinyarwanda; but now, with many Rwandans returning after decades of living in exile in Burundi and Uganda, there was no unifying language. There was a huge population shift – many familiar friends having fled or been killed and others arrived in their place. Would I find anyone I knew? What of Charles's family – had any of them survived? Would I be able to find them?

Three weeks before we were due to leave, I made a phone call to another British colleague from Rwanda who had recently returned. He had been to Butare and spoken directly with the bishop there. He confirmed, although the details were slightly different, that Charles had indeed been taken away by the military, and was presumed shot:

Friday, 9 September
I guess he's probably right. I suppose it can't be any other way. Yet *again* the grief hits me as it has done so many times before. Yet even now it's still not definite. I still need to go back and find out. But will I find out any more? Should I not just accept what I've been told as being final? It is SO hard. I mourn for him and weep, most of me saying 'that's it' – yet part of me saying 'what if . . .?'

On a human level, I can't believe the sadness that has been mine over this last year. But my tragedy seems relatively small compared to that of so many Rwandans, having lost not just one but many of their family. And it reminds me of how cushy life is for most in the West, where we don't expect suffering to be a normal part of life. So different from our African brethren – and especially from Jesus.

Surely such suffering and pain is only to be expected in this life. This world isn't home for any of us. We're only here for a short time. Charles isn't actually dead. His body may have no life left in it where it's lying in the forest somewhere. But he's been given a new body now in Heaven, a perfect one, and he's happier now than he's ever been before. All his fear, pain, distress – everything to do with darkness – it's all gone now . . .

Or was it? That was what I was determined to find out.

7

Return to Rwanda

By the end of September 1994, the phones in Rwanda were beginning to work again. It was now almost six months since I had had direct contact with anyone inside the country, so a working phone system seemed good news. But who was there left to phone? Charles and I had no phone, and most of those I knew with phones had either been killed or had fled the country.

Of Charles's family, I still had no news whatsoever. I had last spoken to his older sister Diane on the phone from Kenya just days before the killing broke out. After that I tried several times to make contact with her, but there was never any reply. I had imagined the worst, then the phones were cut off completely.

Now I was afraid to try to call her. Surely they would all have been killed, their house destroyed. Or perhaps they just might be still alive, but have fled. Probably someone would have taken over their house in Kigali. Was there any point in phoning? But I knew I had to do it. I had to find out what had happened, even if it was bad.

My hands were shaking as I tapped out the numbers on the phone. The connection was made straight away. I could hear the long single tone 'beeeeeeeeep ...

beeeeeeeep', so at least their phone was working. After only two or three rings, someone answered it.

'Allo?'

So I was right, was my immediate thought. Someone has moved into their house. I could not imagine they could possibly be still in their own home.

'Allo. Are Diane or Christophe there please?' I tried in my best Kinyarwandan to ask for Charles's sister and brother-in-law.

The reply on the other end of the phone astounded me. 'Just a minute please. I'll go and call them.' Was it possible? Were they really there?

'Allo?' A man's voice was speaking to me.

'Is that Christophe?'

'Yes.'

'Christophe Nduwayo?' My voice was rising with excitement. I could hardly believe that my brother-in-law had not only survived, but was even in his own home!

He was confused by my questioning. 'This is Christophe Nduwayo. Who am I speaking to?'

'IT'S LESLEY!!!' I squealed down the phone to him.

In the course of the conversation I learned that his whole family had survived – his wife Diane and their eight children – and they were now back together in their own home. They had heard nothing whatsoever of Charles, except that his clerical collar and a photo album had been discovered in the home of a close friend in Butare.

'We are assuming he must have been killed,' he told me gravely. 'If he were still alive, he would have made contact with us by now.'

My heart sank; this was the news I had been dreading. I had held out hope on the basis that those who had brought me the rumours of his death might simply not know where he was, but if his immediate family had heard no news, there was very little hope now.

There was no time to ask news of all the family over the telephone, but I told him when we would be arriving at Kigali airport, and he promised they would be there to meet us.

My mind was swirling as I put down the phone. How *wonderful* to know that they had survived and that I would be seeing them again soon. And how marvellous that they would be there to talk over much of what had happened. They were straightforward, God-fearing Catholic people. I knew I could trust them. And that would be so important in a land where so many had betrayed and been betrayed, where friend, neighbour and colleague could no longer be trusted.

But what of this news of Charles? How did that leave me feeling? In a strange kind of way, I felt almost a sense of relief. The uncertainty of not knowing had often been almost intolerable, and the hope of finding him alive had become increasingly slim. And yet I could not give up on that little hope I still had. But now, with his close family saying that they no longer held out any hope, I would have to accept that he most probably had been killed.

So the month travelling around Rwanda would not now be spent searching, asking, and being disappointed again and again. The time for agonising over the uncertainty of the last six months was over. It was now time to acknowledge the reality of the facts, and to begin to grieve for the almost certain loss of my husband. It was a bitter realisation, but it was also strangely helpful.

*

Our transport arrangements to Rwanda began as they were to continue – notoriously unreliable. A half-hour delay in our flight from London to Nairobi meant that the small six-seater that should have taken Jennifer and me on to Kigali left without us, and it took us two days in Nairobi to find another plane with space for two passengers.

My face was pressed hard against the window as we flew low over Rwanda. I soaked in the familiar and beautiful sight of a carpet of rolling hills below us, each one speckled with tiny homesteads, fields and green banana patches. But as we dropped our height and I could see more details of the scene below, the twinges of excitement and familiarity usually associated with a return to Rwanda were quickly smothered. It was not just the destruction that distressed me – the burnt-out shells that had once been beautiful villas, or the piles of rubble in the middle of a row of simple mud houses. There was something else very strange about this whole scene: there were no people in sight, not one. The land looked totally abandoned. This 'land of a thousand hills', until April the most densely populated country in Africa, was deserted.

Thus it was with a mixture of excitement and fear, joy and intense sadness, a sense of homecoming yet feeling a stranger, that I chatted my way through immigration and customs formalities. As the original plans that Jennifer and I had made had not worked out, there was no one to meet us. So we hitched a lift into town with the Red Cross, with whom we had flown from Nairobi.

Driving along the main road, the signs of conventional war were very evident. Many buildings were peppered with bullet holes and a few had been badly damaged. Yet much worse, and more sinister, was the damage in the residential areas. Individual houses had clearly been specifically targeted and totally destroyed, while other houses around remained untouched.

Unlike the empty countryside, here in the city there were plenty of people around – and also a remarkable number of vehicles. The majority seemed to be huge white four-wheel drive pick-ups and Land Rovers, displaying a whole host of different aid-agency insignias. But as I looked more closely, I realised that most of the rest bore either a Burundian or a Ugandan registration plate, their owners being some of the thousands of Rwandan exiles who had now returned to their homeland.

Having found somewhere to stay for the night, my first priority was to contact Charles's family. Jennifer and I had no transport and were still unsure of the security situation, particularly at night, so Christophe offered to collect us. Amazingly, they still had their old, battered pick-up truck. We learned that the militia, while stealing it out of their drive, had crashed it into the wall and abandoned it – so it was still there when my brother-in-law returned home at the end of the war!

It was already dark by the time we set off for their house; I felt quite nervous to be out in the streets, though it was still early. Christophe reassured us that there was nothing to worry about; it was now quite safe. Certainly, there were many more people on the streets now than I had seen in the months preceding the war.

Charles's sister Diane was waiting for us. Without a word she opened the door and we clasped each other tightly. For a few seconds there was silence; the silence of a shared grief that was too deep, too painful, for any words. There are no words in any language that can express the depth of emotion that we and so many others felt. I wanted to cry, but knew that would not be acceptable, so somehow managed to hold back my tears.

As each member of the household came through to greet us, we learned exactly how not only Diane and Christophe had survived, but also their eight children. With the help of Hutu friends, who risked their lives to protect them, and by the grace of God, they had separated and gone different ways. Christophe, aware that he would be searched out and targeted, instructed his wife and children to flee, while he remained in the house. 'If they come to look for me and don't find me, they'll kill all of you,' he had told his family. 'I'll stay here so that they can kill me, and perhaps they'll not bother to look for you.' Yet throughout the war each member of the family was kept safe and was gradually reunited with the others in their almost undamaged home after the RPF took over Kigali.

Charles also had a younger sister in Kigali, recently married, and with small twins. Her husband had been outside their house one day early on in the war, when he was approached by a man with his head and face covered, machete in hand. The militia was looking for a man by the name of Claude. Did my brother-in-law happen to know where he lived?

Did he know? He knew all right. That was his own name! He managed to respond calmly that he knew of no such person in the area, and the militia left. But that more than convinced him that he must seek a safe place for himself, his wife and children. Once again, with the help of trusted Hutu friends, they were moved safely to one of the large hotels that was being protected by

UN troops. They had to pay a huge sum of money to be allowed the privilege of staying there, even though for most people the only alternative was almost certain death. They also had to find some way of buying food, which became increasingly difficult. As the weeks wore on, the food supplies dwindled. The little that they had they gave to the twins, and at times they went for days without eating anything themselves.

Yet they survived, while so many did not. Claude knew of only three members of his extended family who had survived – out of a total of over two hundred. I could hardly begin to grasp the enormity of that. I tried to imagine losing *all* of my brothers and sisters, my parents, my nieces and nephews, aunts, uncles, cousins. *All* of them – except two. It was too horrific to take in.

For those who did not live in the capital, the situation had been very bleak indeed. Charles's father and step-mother, an elderly, kind-hearted couple, had lived in a rural area outside Kigali, where the killings had been particularly barbaric. They had fled, together with Juliette, the third of Charles's sisters, and her four children, to their local church to seek sanctuary.

It had not been difficult for the army and militia to break down the doors there, so those who were not blown up by the grenades thrown through the windows were then hacked to death by machete. Juliette's youngest son was still strapped to her back when he was clubbed to death by a heavy stick with nails in it. Perhaps they thought she too was dead, as she lay motionless among the thousands of corpses on the church floor. All four of her children were murdered, along with her father and her stepmother. She alone survived.

But at what cost.

I did not see Juliette as she had returned to the family home. Or rather, to what had been the family home, for there was virtually nothing left standing. It had all been destroyed except one small hut in the backyard that still had a roof. They were hoping one day to repair it, but with no income it would take a very long time. I wanted to go there to visit her, but was told that the main bridge across the river had been blown up and that the alternative route was a very lengthy detour.

Most of the time I sat stunned, listening to these horrific experiences. When I felt I could take no more I turned to Jennifer to translate what I could bear to repeat. Relating the stories in English somehow seemed to make them even more vivid, though.

As the evening wore on, the room began to fill up with people. Some were friends who had come to visit. That in itself seemed strange, since before the war most people had been too afraid to walk about in town much after six-thirty, when it got dark. Others were long-lost relatives who had returned to Rwanda from Uganda, some of whom had never before set foot in Rwanda. I remembered seeing Charles's photographs of relatives in Uganda, whom he had known during his school-days and teacher training years. Now here they were – but the person who had brought us together was not with us.

As I talked with an aunt who sat beside me, I realised that she was the one who had been like a surrogate mother to Charles when he first went to Uganda in his early teens. She had not seen him since he returned to Rwanda in the mid-1980s, and had never met me, his wife. She was clearly profoundly moved by the situ-

ation and she could say very little. When I produced a
recent photo of Charles, that was more than she could
handle. Pushing the photo away, she turned her head
to the side and, with most untypically Rwandan
emotion, I could see her eyes fill up with tears. I too
fought back my own.

Many, many times during the evening I became
acutely conscious that someone was missing in our
midst. It was Charles alone who had brought me into
contact with this family. I had no other reason to be
there; but he was not here.

Charles's two brothers and three sisters had all survived. So why did he have to die, the only one among
the siblings? Why was he not here among us now? It
seemed so totally unfair and unjust. Why, oh why? But
at least they had survived; I was so grateful for that.

We talked of Charles and I explained the various
pieces of news that I had been given. It was the first
time they had heard any details of his journey to Butare
and what happened to him there, but it fitted with the
news they had received from his friend there.

By this time I knew I had to go to Butare to find out
for myself, and I was glad when Diane expressed a
willingness to come with me. It would be such a painful
visit for both of us. As we spent time praying together
before leaving, I realised how grateful I was for these
people. Not only had they welcomed and supported
me as their sister-in-law since the beginning of our
marriage (something many families would not do for
their in-laws), but even now they were still including
me and trusting me as one of their family. It was a
great privilege for me, and I was glad that we would
have more time to spend together over the next month.

*

The house where we stayed for our first two nights in Kigali had previously been the home of a British missionary family, but was now being used by the Episcopal Church. Shell damage to the roof, walls and windows had mostly been repaired, although the walls were still peppered with bullet holes. It was a great luxury to discover that not only was there now electricity in this part of the city, but also working telephones, running water, and even a flush toilet.

Stepping into the bathroom for the first time I was suddenly and starkly reminded of our bathroom at home in Gahini. Positive, but inexplicable, feelings flooded through me. I could not understand why, until I noticed the half-used bar of pink 'Claire' soap on the basin. This was the locally made soap with a very distinctive perfume that we had always used. Once again, it was the smells that evoked the most vivid memories.

In the morning we walked into town. Considering the country was emerging from a genocide, there was a remarkable number of people around and a surprising air of normality. There were builders balancing on treacherous-looking scaffolding, repairing some of the damaged buildings; ladies in groups of six or eight, sweeping up the broken glass and rubbish that had lain undisturbed for months at the sides of the roads. Many of the small shops and cafés were open again for business. Some I recognised, some I did not. Some had been shops, now turned into cafés; others had been cafés, now turned into shops. Some now had English names – almost unheard of before the war in this ex-Belgian protectorate.

We stood across the road from the post office. Some sections were functioning, but it was not yet receiving

or sending mail. Damage to the mail sorting section
from a grenade blast some months before the war had
only just been repaired, and now here it was – out of
action once again. Oh what tragedy this little country
has known, again and again.

We needed to change some dollars into local Rwandan francs, but the two banks we had passed were
clearly not yet operative. As we stood pondering what
to do, a young man came bounding across the road
towards us. I recognised him instantly – 'Ziggi' they
called him – one of the waiters from a local restaurant
where I used to buy a cheap lunch on trips into Kigali.
But Ziggi also had another job on the side – changing
money on the black market for tourists. I had never
made use of his services, but he had always been very
chatty, hopeful perhaps that I might bring him some
clients from the regular foreign visitors we received.

Ziggi and I greeted one another as long lost friends,
exchanging the news of the past six months. Very
quickly a small crowd gathered, including some of the
handicapped men who used to hang around town,
offering to guard a vehicle in exchange for a few francs.

Ziggi took me by the arm, drawing me away a little
from the crowd, and began to talk in hushed tones. 'So
you want to exchange some dollars? You won't find
any banks working, you know. Everyone has to buy
from us. But I'll give you a good rate – because you are
my friend.' I had no choice, and at least I could be
reasonably confident that he would not cheat me.
Across the road were another twenty or thirty money-
changers, each with their plastic bags full of dollars,
and thousands and thousands of Rwandan francs
stuffed into their pockets.

'Are you not afraid of thieves?' I asked him as I

searched for my dollars. 'There's so much money over there – and so obvious!'

He took the notes and began to examine them carefully. 'No one would dare touch any of us. All the rest would kill him,' he replied. I could well imagine that. These were all hefty guys – I would certainly not like to get on the wrong side of any of them!

During the evening a number of visitors came to visit our host. One of these couples, James and Annette, I had known a little before, and had heard something of their escape, but was keen to hear the details. We were in a delicate situation. We certainly did not want to cause pain to anyone by asking them to relate their experiences to us. On the other hand, we were finding that many people were more than ready to speak to us in great detail, and without any prompting.

Certainly that was the case with James. He and his family were Tutsis who had lived and worked in Kigali for a number of years. James was quite convinced that God had protected him, his wife and four children, and was therefore ready and willing to tell anyone. But it was not all good news for him. As far as he was aware, every single member of his family had been killed, and his mother had been burned alive. James certainly did not take his own survival lightly. Yet he sensed that God had a purpose in sparing him, and he was ready to respond to whatever God called him to do.

He had decided to flee from his home in Kigali, together with his wife and children, when he realised that as an educated Tutsi his life was in danger. They went to the home of some foreign friends, but very soon these people were evacuated, leaving James and his family alone in the house. 'We spent much of our time hiding in a walk-in cupboard in the kitchen, in the pitch black,' he explained, 'terrified that the house would be searched. In fact, it was searched, but the door opening into the kitchen completely covered over the door to our cupboard, and no one even realised we were in there!'

As I wondered about the near impossibility of trying to keep three small children and a baby quiet in a pitch-black cupboard, he carried on. 'We had run out of food in the house. The children were hungry, and we were stuck in this cupboard, too afraid to go out, yet knowing we might eventually have to or we would starve. At one point I heard something fall on the floor in front of me. I bent down to discover what it was, and held it to my nose as I could see nothing. It smelt like chocolate, so I tasted it. It *was* chocolate! I reached my hand up to the shelf above my head, and found it was full of Swiss chocolate! So for the next few days we lived off Swiss chocolate!'

'But you couldn't survive without water. Where did you get water from?' I asked.

'When it rained hard,' James replied, 'it was so noisy on the roof that we couldn't be heard, and no one goes out in the rain, so we sent one of the children out to collect rain water. Being small, even if they were noticed, they wouldn't attract much attention.'

'So what happened when you had finished all the chocolate?'

'The day after the chocolate ran out, a shell fell in the garden and there was a terrific crash. We were terrified, and thought our time was up. But during the next rain we went to look and saw that the explosion had felled an avocado tree – right outside our door! So for the next week or so we ate avocados and drank water.

'After that we really thought we would starve. The fighting in the city was getting worse and worse, and there was no way we could go out to get food. But we didn't need to. One morning we looked out and there outside the door was a carpet of tiny white mushrooms! One of the children went out to gather them and we ate them straight away. The next day they were there again, another carpet. And do you know, the funny thing was that if we kept them overnight, by the next morning they were full of worms. So we had to eat them all up each day. And yet every day more had grown in their place.'

We were amazed. 'Wow! It's just like God providing manna for the Israelites in the wilderness. That was white too, and was full of worms if they kept it till the next day.'

'Have you written all this down, James?' Jennifer asked. 'You know, it's really important that people know these things. It would be a great encouragement to Christians around the world who have been praying for the Rwandans throughout this crisis.'

We felt it a great privilege to be with these people; to share their enthusiasm for the Lord and their gratitude to him. There were to be many gruesome experiences related to us over the weeks to come, and of course many, many people hadn't had a miraculous escape such as that of James's family. But it was tremendous to hear the good news too. However dark and hopeless a situation may be, I had begun to learn that there is always something good that can come out of it. And here, sitting talking with us, was living proof of that.

The next day, we had arranged to go to Gahini. In the still volatile situation within the country, public transport was not advisable, so we were grateful to be offered a lift – even if it meant the visit would have to be quite short.

The road was very quiet all the way, hardly a car, and very few people. Most of the houses along the roadside were deserted, some of them completely razed to the ground, with the grass beginning to grow over the piles of earth that had once been homes. The fields of sorghum and maize in the valleys were choked with weeds, and huge sticks of bananas hung ready to cut in the overgrown banana patches. It was all so familiar – and yet now so different.

The road sloped gently downhill from Kayonza and bent round towards the river in the valley, and Lake Muhazi. With the green, gently rolling hills in the background, it was a truly beautiful sight. Yet as we approached the bridge across the river, a shiver ran down my spine. I had never smelt this smell before, but I knew it immediately as the acrid bitterness hit the back of my nose and my throat; it was like nothing else on earth. The stench of rotting human flesh. Six months ago bound and mutilated human beings had been tossed into this river and lake in their hundreds, perhaps even thousands, just like a farmer would throw the banana skins to his pigs. Six months on, the bitter stench still lingered in the air, a constant reminder of death.

I looked at Jennifer. 'Do you realise what that smell is?' She too had guessed. Perhaps those who lived there had grown used to it by now. Young children were down at the water's edge filling their jerrycans to take home. What a health nightmare, but they had no alternative.

We said nothing more, but drove on. As the great

expanse of the lake came into view I remembered
reading some of the journalists' reports back in April.
Their awe at the breathtaking beauty of the Rwandan
countryside was matched only by their shock beyond
belief at the atrocities they had to report, taking place
in that very same land.

A few kilometres farther along the side of the lake
we left the tarmac road, turning on to the steep, rough
road up to Gahini, now even more full of pot-holes
than before. My heart was racing as we approached the
top of the hill. Each lane was familiar – each house,
each building, each corner, held memories.

I was trying to point them out to Jennifer all at once.
The big house on the corner where the bishop and his
family had lived, then the long house with bright
yellow doors that had been Charles's before we were
married, and the really old one behind where he had
lived when he first arrived in Gahini. There were the
red-brick state secondary school buildings on the left,
and the environmental health project buildings taken
over as new diocesan offices just a year ago.

We drove on a little farther. 'There's the old Stanley
Smith Bible College on the right, and the primary
school – oh look, that's the church straight in front of
us. And in behind the trees on the left, that's the roof
of our house.' I pointed it all out to Jennifer.

I had a strong urge to jump out of the car and run
straight to our house. I was home! But we drove on,
round past what had been the rehabilitation centre for
handicapped people and up the front drive to the
hospital. The road was now terribly overgrown and
untidy looking, but the hospital itself looked almost the
same – but for one thing.

'But why on earth did they have to destroy Rob's

office?' I asked, as I stared at the shell which had once
been the medical director's office. The smooth cream
outer walls of this section of the hospital were still
standing, and the blue corrugated iron-sheet roofing
had been repaired. Yet the inside had clearly been
devastated – the whole section, containing not only
Rob's office, but administration, statistics, store room
and . . . of course, that was it: Accounts. I had already
found the answer to my own question. It wasn't Rob's
office they were interested in. They wanted to blow the
safes and take the money.

I got out of the car slowly, looking all around me,
trying to take everything in at once. There was only
one person in sight – a young girl in a clean white
hospital coat walking past the front of the building. We
recognised each other at the same moment, and I leapt
up the steps to greet her.

It was Rose, one of the nurses – still here, still
working, still smiling. Not a word was spoken as we
embraced one another. It was a silence that was to
characterise every reunion with friends and family. We
knew each other's trauma. We could identify with one
another's pain. Words would be meaningless.

But there were none the less plenty of questions to
be asked. Rose was keen to explain how things had
been in Gahini, and also to tell me of those who were
still there. With enthusiasm she marched us off round
the back of the main building towards the central area
of the hospital to find some of the other staff whom I
would know.

I noticed how ordinary everything appeared. Patients
sat on the low walls around the wards, watching the
world go by – just as they always had done. Their
carers busied themselves on the grass outside with

scrubbing the clothes, preparing food for lunch, or collecting water – just as it had always been. Yes, even the central water tap was working!

The pharmacy was open and people queued outside to collect their medicines. I peeped into the operating theatre on the way past. 'Those are new pieces of equipment in there,' I commented to Jennifer. 'Those weren't here before.' These were encouraging signs. It was clearly still a well-functioning hospital.

Within minutes of our arrival, the word got round that I was back. The few original staff who were still there appeared one by one to greet me; it was wonderful to see them again. But each one asked the same question – 'Have you come back to stay?' And each time I struggled with the answer. Well, no, I had only come back on a visit, but maybe I would come back again one day. God knew, even if I didn't know yet.

I kept feeling the inequality of the situation. When things were tough, I had been out of the country – and I could stay out as long as the situation remained insecure. It was relatively easy for me. But what else could these people do? Nothing. They had been to hell and back; they had survived. Yet life now was terribly hard for them – and what of their future?

I was keen to stay and listen, but I could sense Rose was a little anxious by the commotion caused around us. White visitors were obviously a relatively rare sight, particularly one who knew people personally and could speak Kinyarwanda.

'I need to take you to meet the medical director – he ought to know you're here,' Rose said.

Anxious not to step out of line, we followed her towards the large open Nutritional Centre building, whose offices our community health programme had shared. To my amazement, we walked straight up to the door of my own office! But as we approached, a young lad, his soldier's uniform falling off him, stood up and barred our way with his gun. He looked only about ten years old, and his eyes were full of fear and sadness.

Rose explained to him that we wanted to meet the medical director, and we were instructed to wait outside. A few minutes later a young man in military uniform appeared and invited us inside. There was an air of confidence and authority about him, but his manner was pleasant.

Once inside, I began to look around me. The office was now almost bare, except for the rough wooden table that had been my desk, now positioned in the centre of the room to receive visitors. There was no sign of our books or equipment, or even the cupboards. There was just one small bookshelf with some old health workers' files, presumably left because they were of no value to anyone else. It did not really feel like my office any more. It all felt weird.

We explained to the young man who we were and why we had come back. He wanted to know which had been our house, since I said I would also like to go there. 'Why do you want to go there?' he asked. 'What's the point? It's empty now, your husband is not there.'

'I know that,' I replied. 'But I just want to see the place again – it holds so many memories for me. Just to go and look around.'

But no, he could not understand why it was that I should want to visit my old home; and when I pushed further, his reply was firm: 'Your house is out of bounds. It is a military zone. It is quite out of the question for you to go there. You may go anywhere else, but not there.'

Yet I was not prepared to give up. As I searched my mind to think of some logical argument to persuade this man of the harmlessness of our mission, Jennifer suddenly remembered the papers. Yes, that was worth a try: the official papers we had obtained from the RPF prior to coming, promising us assistance and co-operation in our search for Charles. Perhaps official documents from a higher authority might have some influence.

We produced the papers and gave them to him to look at. He took some time to read them through, and then asked if he might keep them as he would need to check with his superiors in Kigali. Our hearts sank – that could take weeks. We were here *now*, and wanted to look round today. However, he was not to be persuaded, so reluctantly we accepted his decision and left the papers with him. Perhaps, we thought, we would have more success on our next visit.

Our time in Gahini that day was limited. The man who had brought us in his car had to get back to Kigali soon after lunch, but before that he had some business to do at a school some 5 miles or so beyond Gahini. As it happened, the one person I very much wanted to see lived only a short walk from that school, so we jumped back into the car and set off.

It was Beatrice that I so wanted to meet again. She had worked as a housegirl first for Lionel and Mary, and then part-time for me. But she'd been much more than a housegirl. She was a humble Christian girl, and a great friend. I remembered how sometimes she would arrive late for work (after a two-hour walk) because she had met some refugees on the road and had spent some time using the last 40 francs in her possession to help them to find some food. Or how she and her elderly, almost blind, mother would take a family of orphans into their home because they had no one to care for them. Like Grace, my regular housegirl and precious friend, she never once asked me for anything, although she lived in the poorest of conditions.

From the road it was a good ten-minute walk to her house, along twisty paths through fields and banana patches. As we got near the beginning of the path I was beginning to wonder if I would remember my way when we passed an elderly gentleman on the road whom I recognised as being from Gahini. I waved furiously at him from the car, and motioned to him to follow. To my relief he did so, and arrived only moments after we stopped the car.

We followed him in single file, pushing back the overgrown bushes that almost blocked the path in places. The whole area was choked with weeds, with only a few heads of overripe sorghum poking over the top of them.

'Why don't people look after the land any more?' I asked as we walked along.

'There aren't many of us left here in the countryside,' he replied. 'And most of them are too discouraged.'

'But how are they going to live if they don't cultivate?' I said. For most Rwandans, this was their life – sowing, weeding, harvesting and eating the crops. Many had no other source of income. If for any reason the crops failed, then malnutrition, acute poverty and death were the unavoidable result. For a Rwandan not to cultivate, he or she must be very discouraged indeed.

'Oh they'll find food. There's enough around,' he said.

By now we had reached Beatrice's house, but it looked ominously shut up. I had had no contact with her since leaving back in March, so did not even know if she was still alive. Our guide, though, assured me that she was still very much alive – just not around at the moment. So we went to ask at her neighbour's house, some hundred yards or so away. They told us that Beatrice had gone to work in their fields and her frail old mother had gone to collect firewood. Seeing us approach, the neighbour had immediately sent two of her children to tell them of our arrival.

It was not long before I heard a call: 'She's coming.'

We rushed out and could see in the distance the stooped form of Beatrice's mother, a heavy load of firewood on her head. I began to run towards her, but while I was still some distance away she fell to her knees, her load tumbling on to the ground. Thinking she was ill, or had perhaps collapsed under the weight, I speeded up. Despite her thick glasses, she had always told us that her eyesight was so poor she could hardly see, so I did not think she could possibly have recognised me from such a distance.

But the small crowd that had by this time gathered began to laugh. 'Yamumenye! Dore, yamumenye! She has recognised her! Look, she has recognised her!'

Sure enough, there was nothing wrong with the old lady – she was simply overcome with emotion. I helped her to her feet as the others caught up, and she grasped me so tightly I thought I might burst! By this time we were all laughing – except Beatrice's mother, who was half-muttering, half-sobbing, and still holding on to me very tightly.

As we headed back towards the house, Beatrice appeared from the opposite direction. She stood motionless in the open yard, her hands covering her face. I ran up to her and threw my arms around her. She buried her head into my shoulder and cried.

'Hey, don't cry, Beatrice. What's up?' She was trying to control her emotions, but not succeeding very well.

'I thought you were dead,' she whispered into my ear. 'I thought they had killed you too.'

I hugged her again as the tears began to trickle down my cheeks too. As we walked back towards her little mud house, she explained.

'When things began to quieten down a bit I went back to Gahini. I walked along the road beside the *Bazungu* homes looking to see if anyone was around. I didn't see anyone I knew, but I asked a man on the road, "Where are the people who used to live in these houses?" He told me that some of them had fled and others had been killed. So I thought you must have been killed. After that I didn't want to go back to Gahini again. I haven't been there since April.'

'But Beatrice, had you forgotten that I had gone to Kenya?'

She looked at me and paused. 'Yes, I had forgotten.'

We went in through the back door of their little house and into the darkness of the sitting-room. The tiny wooden window was closed and the only source of light was from the open back door. There were a few rickety wooden chairs on the uneven earth floor, and a hefty wooden cupboard in the corner.

'Look, aren't we well off?' Beatrice was laughing by this time. 'We've even got some furniture! We fled into the Park [the Akagera National Wildlife Park] when the killing started round here, but then we came back home after two weeks. Our house had been emptied, but there was furniture lying around all over the hills, just abandoned. So we took a few things, just to replace what we had lost.' Sure enough, they had nothing fancy, just the basics they had had before.

We sat for an hour or so, crouched on the low chairs, one minute joining in with Beatrice's infectious laugh, the next agonising over some of the sad news. Her mother may have had better sight than she had led us to believe, but her hearing was not what it used to be, and many of the questions and tales were repeated several times for her benefit.

Like those tales of the man who wandered into the house in the middle of our conversations. I was initially wary of his presence, having never seen him before, but the ladies were quite unperturbed by him. He described himself to us as 'the man who came back from the dead', and when he took off his cap to reveal a huge scar across his head I could understand why. He related to us how he had been taken to the edge of a pit in which were already hundreds of dead bodies, and then hacked over the back of his head with a machete. Some hours later he recovered his senses and found himself lying in the pit among the bodies. It was some time before he realised that he was actually alive, and then somehow found the strength to climb out.

So for some reason God had preserved his life – but had not saved Charles. And yet, while I longed that it should be Charles sitting opposite me relating this amazing tale of survival, I could not help but think that Charles was in fact the better off of the two of them. Life in these days was tough for this man and his future extremely uncertain; but in heaven, Charles was now free from all worries and fears of the present and future.

Because she no longer worked for the expatriates, Beatrice spent her days working in their fields with her mother. Her own comfort had never been a priority for her in the past, and neither was it now. Even though they had so little between them, they still shared with those in greater need around them – with children who had been orphaned, with those who were ill, with women who had lost their husbands. We spent some time praying for these people, and I said how I hoped to come back and stay for a few days when Beatrice could take me to meet some of them. It would be so good to have some time to spend with the people here.

For the meantime, though, our schedule was dictated by our Western lifestyle: our watches. Beatrice and her mother were very reluctant to let us leave, particularly as they had not even had time to make a drink for us, let alone a meal. They absolutely insisted that we must come back again for a meal, and even to stay.

As we left the house through the backyard, Beatrice scooped a handful of what looked like dark brown crumbs out of a basket on the ground. 'Smell this,' she said, holding her hand up to my nose. 'Do you recognise it?'

I took a deep sniff at the contents of her hand. 'It's coffee!'

She burst out laughing and slapped me on the back. 'You see, we've become *Bazungu* now! We can't buy tea any longer so we roast and grind our own coffee.'

Very few Rwandans drank coffee, although it was one of their main export crops. They always drank tea. I used to laugh at Beatrice and Grace for their strange habit of putting a spoonful of diluted coffee into their tea, because they 'liked the smell, but not the taste'! Now here she was drinking nothing but coffee – and the leftovers at that, having first sifted out the finest, purest grains for selling.

It was hard to say goodbye, but our lift was waiting for us.

As we spoke to more people in and around Gahini I was surprised to find myself feeling increasingly at ease. Perhaps it was not only Kigali that was more secure now. Even the idea of taking a 'minibus' taxi on my own and coming back to stay for a few days sounded perfectly feasible and appealed to me very much. Yes, leaving Gahini was not so painful, I thought, knowing I would be back before too long.

However, I was very soon to find that sense of security and normality severely shaken.

8

Benaco

It was some days before I was able to return to Gahini. First there were two more places I wanted to visit: one was Butare, the town where Charles had last been seen alive; and the other was Benaco, the refugee camp in Tanzania. Not that I had any hope of finding Charles there, but I so much wanted to meet up again with my housegirl Grace, Etienne and Emeralde, my Rwandan family, and other friends from Gahini.

However, finding some means of getting to either place was proving much more difficult than I had imagined. Eventually we negotiated a lift with a convoy of aid lorries travelling to Tanzania, and in the absence of anything more comfortable we gratefully accepted. Thus the following morning we were ready and waiting at the aid agency's headquarters in Kigali, a luxurious whitewashed house with luscious green lawns sprawling down the hillside on several levels. It had clearly been a very comfortable private house prior to the war; but, like so many properties, had now been taken over by newcomers – in this case, a foreign aid agency.

It was an added bonus to discover that spaces had been found for us in the accompanying Land Rover, so our journey would be a little more comfortable. We did not leave until early afternoon, and with a three-hour journey ahead of us on the Rwandan side, it was debatable if we would make it to the border before it closed at five o'clock. Certainly it would be dark before we had completed our journey on the Tanzanian side.

For the first hour the road was the same as the one we had travelled on to Gahini, but at the Kayonza roundabout we turned right and headed due south towards Kibungo town and beyond to Tanzania. The nearer we came to the border, the emptier the countryside became. Small clusters of houses by the roadside stood empty, their doors gently swinging open in the hot breeze to reveal overturned chairs and abandoned personal belongings. They were just as they had been left months ago when their occupiers had fled.

At various places along the side of the road I noticed groups of three large stones together – stones that had served as supports for the cooking pots, as groups of refugees prepared some food where they stopped for the night. It was along this road that Etienne and Emeralde and their children had walked, together with Granny and all her other grandchildren, and Grace – and literally hundreds of thousands of other refugees. Days and days on the road, a few meagre possessions on their heads, walking for hours on end in the roasting sun.

I remembered Etienne's brief description of the journey to me in his very first letter from Benaco. There was no trace of anger or resentment at what had happened to them – just a gratitude to God for bringing them safely to Tanzania. I remembered his sadness at having to abandon his cows on the journey (especially 'my' one) when the fighting came very close, and his simple trust that God would provide more cows for them one day.

Also along the roadside at regular intervals were the remains of branches or parts of felled trees – the last remnants of hastily erected road blocks. These had been manned by militia whose purpose was to sift out the Tutsis and kill them. I tried to imagine how it must have felt to flee in such circumstances, terrified of being singled out, weak and hungry from days without food, fevered with malaria because of sleeping out. Yet there were no complaints in the letters. Instead they spoke of how God comforted them and how the words of the Psalms became so real and relevant to them. 'In those terrible times God showed us the words of Psalms 91 and 125,' Etienne had written only one month after arriving in the refugee camp. 'And we know that in all of this we are surrounded and kept by his angels.' These Rwandan refugees had an understanding and experience of God that very few of us in our comfort and security of the West could even begin to approach.

We reached the border in good time and completed the passport controls without any problems. It was about five years since I had been here. I had come on a picnic with Etienne and Emeralde, together with various family members and friends – all squashed into a clapped-out old car. It was a beautiful spot to visit. We had walked across the bridge joining Rwanda to Tanzania, and marvelled at the brown and frothy waters of the Kagera rushing over the waterfall to the swirling pools far below.

But as I walked towards the border bridge this time, my mind was filled with more recent images. This scene had appeared all too often on our television screens as bloated bodies tumbled down over the waterfall and bobbed about in the pools at the bottom. Sometimes there had been as many as one every minute – hundreds each day. Just being there and thinking about what had happened made me feel sick.

There were no bodies there now, but strewn all down the steep banks by the side of the bridge were pieces of clothing, and numerous *ingata* – rings made of grass or banana leaves, used for carrying things on heads. In the few hours between the former Rwandan army abandoning the border post and the RPF taking it over, hundreds of thousands of people had crammed across that narrow little bridge. Clearly, many had not made it.

Now it was eerily quiet. The only sign of life, apart from the border guards in their barren office, was a small rickety table under the shade of a tree, where a couple of young men sold Fantas and bananas.

We were not allowed to walk across the bridge, and we thought it wiser to keep our cameras firmly inside our bags, so we piled back into the Land Rover and headed for the Tanzanian border post. Here there were three different offices at which we had to check in, each one more shabby and with a more pungent stink of bats than the previous one. To our dismay we discovered that one of the officials had already left. It was five minutes past five, Tanzanian time. The other officials shrugged their shoulders and pointed at their watches. We left it to the man in charge of our convoy to do the talking.

Eventually, after much arguing, and remarkably without the handover of any money, the missing official appeared and our papers were duly completed. Had we been travelling independently and not part of this aid convoy, I had the distinct feeling that we would have ended up staying the night in our car.

By the time we eventually reached our destination, it was dark. We were to be staying in Murgwanza, which until May 1994 had been a small country community similar to Gahini. Now it had been totally changed, overrun by numerous aid agencies, each with their white jeeps and Land Rovers roaring along the mud roads.

The refugees had had to pass through here on their journey over from Rwanda, but were encouraged to continue walking farther inland. They were now camped about one hour's drive from this village. The next morning we would go with the team to the camp, and I would be able to meet up with my friends.

When we had begun to plan this trip some weeks previously, I had hoped to spend a few days in the camp and stay with my family in their little grass shack. However, as I listened to the conversations between some of the team members over the supper table that night, I began to feel distinctly uneasy about the idea.

Security within the camp was not good. Most of the aid agencies had moved their accommodation bases out of the main camp to safer places, and all expatriate staff had to leave the camp by four o'clock in the afternoon. There were also rumours flying around that the militia, who had carried out the genocide but fled as refugees when the RPF took over the country, were secretly training and preparing for a renewed attack on Rwanda. It was said that they wanted to 'finish the job' (that of annihilating all Tutsis as well as any Hutu political opposition) and the date for the attack was rumoured to be 15 October 1994 – only one week away.

I heard tales of Tutsi orphans, or unaccompanied minors as they were called, being murdered in the camp; and even that day, emergency messages had come across on the two-way radios (which everyone had to carry for security) that a Red Cross compound within one of the smaller camps had been attacked.

By the time we were on the road the following morning heading for the camp, I was feeling extremely nervous. Far from contemplating the idea of staying there overnight, I wondered if I would even be safe to set foot in the place. Back in June, I had been warned by Rwandan friends that I should not return to Rwanda or I would be killed. As the wife of a Tutsi, I was also considered a Tutsi. Now, however, the power in Rwanda had changed hands, and those who may have sought my life were living here in Benaco; I felt as though I was driving into a lion's den.

As we drew nearer to the camp the countryside began to change. From being wild and green, the hillsides dotted with trees and shrubs – very similar, I thought, to areas in the National Wildlife Park in Rwanda – it was becoming increasingly bare. Stumps took the place of trees, and the vegetation was drier and browner. Everything that could be burned had been gathered up for the thousands of cooking fires lit each day.

But as we rounded another bend in the road, the view in front of me was like nothing else I had ever seen. Stretching out before us, as far as the eye could see, was a vast expanse of barrenness. It was as though the hillsides and valleys in front of us had some disease: they were speckled all over with tiny dots, thousands and thousands of them, mostly brownish grey, but with a sprinkling of blue. Above them all hung a low layer of heavy smoke. There was not a tree or a piece of vegetation in sight.

The nearer we drove, the busier the roads became; there were people everywhere. Our driver had to creep along very slowly, carefully steering a path through the crowds on the road in front of us. I sat in the back of the Land Rover between two others, wearing dark glasses to hide my face. Every person looked menacing and threatening to me, and I dared not look anyone in the eye for fear that I might be recognised. If it was true that I should have been murdered in Rwanda, then it would only need one person to recognise me and call out 'Tutsi' and within seconds the car would be surrounded and I would be finished – or so I feared. I seriously wondered if I had not made a very big mistake by coming here.

It was a huge relief when eventually we approached the Christian Outreach/Tear Fund Alliance team base on the top of Musuhura Hill on the outskirts of the camp. The camps were being organised according to geographical area within Rwanda. So people from Kibungo town were in one area, people from Gahini in another, and so on. As it happened, the people from Gahini were among those who had been allocated to Musuhura Hill, so they were living right on the doorstep of the Alliance team base.

The tremendous advantage of that was that some of the Alliance staff had been able to make contact with some of my Rwandan family, so locating them would not be difficult. But there was a downside too. The compound was still being built, and many of the labourers were taken from among the Gahini people, who would of course recognise me immediately.

The gates were opened for us and we drove in,

pulling up outside one of the attractively constructed bamboo and grass huts. I followed the others into the hut where a small meeting was in progress. Not wishing to interrupt them, we waited to the side until the meeting was finished and the people involved had left. I had not recognised any of them. Had they recognised me, I wondered? And if so, would they not have thought it very strange that I did not greet them? Yet I was too afraid.

A little girl of about six sat on a bench to the side, cowering and frightened. It was explained to us that she had been picked up by a member of a relief agency because she 'looked like a Tutsi', and they feared for her safety. She was brought here to the co-ordinator of the Alliance's programme for tracing relatives of such children and the staff were trying to find out the girl's background. However, a mixture of shyness in adult company and fear prevented the girl from saying more than just a few words in an almost inaudible whisper. At every question she shifted uneasily in her seat and looked away. I longed to sit by her, put my arm around her, and talk with her. Yet I did not dare admit to speaking Kinyarwandan, so it was only when the other Rwandans had left that I felt free to talk with her.

It was not long before we were back in the car and heading down to the main camp, to the hospital where Etienne worked. We were entirely dependent on the Alliance team for their guidance and transport, and were very grateful to them for giving us their time out of an otherwise hectic schedule.

As well as accompanying me, Jennifer was also there in her professional capacity as Tear Fund's Director of Personnel. Therefore it was important for her to use these times with team members to hear how they were coping with their demanding situations.

If I had worried about how the local Gahini people would treat me, I had not long to think about it. The first person I saw as we drove through the gates of the hospital compound was Sitefano – a well-known local man whose son had reportedly been one of the ring leaders of the killing machine in Gahini. Without any hesitation he came straight up to me as I climbed out of the vehicle, and greeted me warmly. It was a great relief. He sent someone straight away to tell Etienne that I was here, and while we waited a number of other ex-Gahini staff appeared to greet me from the tents that served as wards and departments.

Etienne, it turned out, was on his day off, so we would have to visit him at home. A bystander offered to direct us there, so we clambered back into the vehicle. I had intentionally not informed them of my plans to visit, just in case it all fell through at the last moment. But I knew they would be around – there was nowhere else for them to go.

Their house was apparently not far from the hospital, but it did seem to be in the most densely populated area. The roads were solid with people. Makeshift wooden and plastic-sheeting stalls lined the edges of the roads, selling anything from fresh meat, to fire-wood, to home-brewed beer. Little businesses offered to cut your hair, sew your clothes, mend your bicycle – all for a price. It was among this sea of people that I suddenly spotted someone I knew.

'Hey stop, stop! That's Francoise!'

Francoise was Emeralde's sister, and had been one of the bridesmaids at our wedding. If I was amazed to pick her out by chance in such a crowd of people, she was absolutely dumbfounded to see me. I did not want to get out of the car here in the heart of the camp, so I leaned over to the window and beckoned her to come. She obviously could not believe her eyes, though, because she stood motionless, holding her hands to her face in amazement. But even in the few seconds she delayed, the crowd was rapidly gathering around the vehicle. We had to move on fast.

'Come on, Francoise! Come here quickly!' She eventually got the message and we bundled her into the car as it quickly moved off. While Francoise and I hugged each other, the others did not know whether to laugh or cry! Fancy just bumping into her at the side of the road, among one-third of a million people!

Just a little farther up the road, our guide instructed us to stop the car. 'It's off the road, just here. Only a minute to walk. It's very close.'

I felt panic. Judging by the commotion we had caused by stopping on the road already, there was no way I was going to get out of the car and walk anywhere! It all felt so oppressive to me. So instead we dropped the man off to go and find them, while we turned around and went straight back to the hospital.

Within just a few minutes Etienne and Emeralde arrived, together with their two oldest and two youngest children. What a reunion! We hugged and hugged each other, Emeralde sobbing quietly as she clung tightly to me. How wonderful it was to be with them again.

Emeralde and the children looked remarkably well, but I was shocked to see how thin and gaunt Etienne had become. He seemed to have aged years in the six months since I had last seen him, but he shrugged off my concerns, blaming it on the malaria rife in the camp. I hoped very much that he was right.

We talked for a few minutes all together, but I could not relax until I had found just one more person – Grace. Fortunately, she too lived close by, so Emeralde went off to find her.

None of the group who were with me will ever forget that reunion. Grace ran towards me with arms outstretched and fell into my arms, burying her head into my chest. She wept and wept until I could feel the tears trickling down the inside of my blouse, and still she wept. I wanted to introduce her to Jennifer, and to Paul and Laura, the two team members who were also with us, but she would not let me go!

I asked for news of her brother and his family with whom she had been living, and she burst into tears again. Fearing that they may have been killed, I turned to ask Emeralde, but she too had begun to cry.

Life was hard for Grace. Not only had there been tensions living with her brother's family, but a younger brother to whom she had been very close suddenly disappeared a year ago. Her closest friend, Beatrice, whom I had visited a few days previously, had stayed behind in Rwanda, and I too had abandoned her to return to the UK. Yet all this sadness and loss in her life had not hardened her; she was still a sensitive and gentle soul. My heart ached for this girl. So many times in the past had I wept with her over her agonies, and now this. But what exactly had happened?

Grace's sister-in-law, I discovered, had continued to make life very difficult for her, as she had done in Rwanda, being rude, shouting at her, making false accusations; and all the more so now because there was no money coming in. The situation had become intolerable, so Grace had left.

Now I too began to cry, and turned to plead with Jennifer. 'Oh, can't we take Grace back with us? I can't leave her here. She has no family now, no one to care.' Jennifer's eyes were also brimming with tears, as were Paul's and Laura's. Suddenly we were all too aware that it was not a 'refugee crisis' that was being dealt with, but individual people. This great mass of desperate, needy and hungry humanity was made up of unique individuals. Each one had his or her own background, relationships, family. Each one was precious – Grace, Etienne, Emeralde, and all the others whose names we did not even know.

Deep down, I knew we could not take Grace back with us. In fact, we could not even take her out of the camp for a night. But having arranged to meet up again with Etienne and Emeralde on Monday, we were driven back to Musuhura Hill where Grace and I could talk quietly. The others had work to see to, so left us alone – with a two-way radio – for two hours. It was a very precious time, chatting, catching up on each other's news and praying together.

The following day was Sunday. On Sundays, the teams do not go into the camps, so we spent the day in Murgwanza. I found this very frustrating. Our time in Tanzania was so short, and I would far rather have spent as much of it as possible with friends in the camps. Yet we could go nowhere without transport and guidance, and because the team needed time to relax there was no choice.

Before arriving in Tanzania I had expected to find being in a refugee camp difficult to come to terms with, but what I had given no thought to was coping with life among the Non Government Organisation (NGO) staff. The two communities were worlds apart. The staff were there to do their job through the day, but in the evenings and Sundays their lives were totally separate – perhaps they had to be in order to survive in such miserable circumstances.

A number of the people in the various aid agencies had worked in some of the worst trouble spots of the world. To some of them, Rwanda was just another Somalia, another Bosnia. For my part, I could not see it that way. Consequently, I declined the offer of accompanying a group of them to the Rusomo Falls for a picnic. How could anyone enjoy the beauty of that spot after the tragedy that had taken place there, and where the remnants of death were still visible for all to see? Instead I relaxed alone outside, swinging gently on a hammock strung in the shade of two trees.

On the following day we returned to the camp, but not immediately. The team members were frantically busy, and there were not sufficient vehicles for everyone, so we had to hang around for quite a while. It was late morning when we eventually got there. Three of the older boys in Etienne's and Emeralde's family were waiting for us outside the gate of the Alliance compound on Musuhura Hill, and immediately left to tell the rest of the family that we had arrived. One by one they appeared and joined our growing group. We sat in a circle on long wooden benches in the cool shelter of one of the bamboo and grass huts. The materials for these huts were purchased locally, then prepared by the refugee women and constructed by the refugee men as part of a community development project. It was a cool and pleasant place where we could talk openly without disturbance.

Not all of the family had come. Little Yakobo and Naome, the two youngest grandchildren in Granny's extended household, were not there. Yakobo was one of my godchildren – and one of my favourites. A cheeky chap, full of mischief, he was the youngest of six siblings and lived with his mother, 'Granny' and the rest of the extended family. His mother, Jeanne, had been one of our most promising health workers. Conscientious, hard-working and caring, she had also been a great practical support to me on many an occasion when entertaining crowds of visitors in our home.

Some years back, though, Jeanne had contracted AIDS and was now very weak. How she made it to the camp, I had no idea, because when I last saw her in Rwanda at the end of March, she had been too weak to get out of bed – let alone walk anywhere. Understandably, she had not come up to see me with the others. She was now much too weak to walk the few hundred yards from their tiny hut to the compound on the top of the hill.

Yakobo and Naome would be joining us later, I was told – they were at school for the morning. However, Marc was here, Etienne's and Emeralde's youngest. I enquired why he too wasn't at school.

'He asked if he could stay off to come and see you,' Emeralde began. 'But we told him he was to go to school and then come along to join us at midday when the school closed. So he went off in the morning, but then sneaked away and ran up the hill to join us!' I sat him on the bench beside me and put my arm around his shoulders as his mother began to describe to us the events of April.

They had not wanted to leave Gahini and run away,

but the situation was becoming increasingly dangerous, both from the frenzied killings of the local militia, and from the growing threat of the approaching RPF army from the north. In the end it was a hurried, last-minute decision on 16 April, ten days after the president's plane was shot down and the murdering had begun.

It had seemed as though all of Gahini was leaving en masse. They had quickly bundled together a few belongings, rolled up a couple of mattresses, and fixed them on to the back of Etienne's bicycle. Etienne's elderly mother had set off with them, but before long they realised that in her frailty and confusion she was not going to be able to keep up with them. So she returned home alone.

'There were thousands and thousands of us,' Emeralde continued. 'We were all walking together down the road towards Kayonza, thinking that soon we would be able to go back home again. We really never imagined we would have to come this far.'

'Was the family all together?' I asked.

'Yes. We had met at Granny's, and all headed off together. God did a miracle in Jeanne's life. Do you remember how weak she was when you last saw her?' I remembered very well. She was suffering from severe diarrhoea and malaria, and I had not expected to see her again after my two-week holiday in Kenya.

'Well, amazingly, she was given the strength to walk with us,' Emeralde said. 'She didn't carry anything, but she was the one who was encouraging us and cheering us along.

'After we had been on the road for two days, someone arrived with our cows, because they didn't think we should have left them behind. That night one of the cows gave birth and Jeanne carried the little calf on her

shoulders for the next few days! Can you believe that
she should have the strength to do that! We had not
brought any food with us, but we were able to buy a
little on the roadside along the way. But sometimes we
had to walk a long way to search for water.

'On one occasion after several days on the road, there
were rumours that the RPF was getting closer and
people began to panic. We were hungry and thirsty.
We had lost the cows in the panic, and one of the
mattresses, and we really felt we could not go on any
longer. I remembered a Christian friend who lived in
the area where we were, but some distance from the
road. We were not happy about leaving the main road
on our own, in case things were worse in the countryside, but we decided just to go and ask her if we could
rest for a day or two in her home.

'She was like an angel from heaven to us. Since her
husband had died she had set aside a large room in her
house as a prayer room, and she told us it was now
ours – a room for the people of God. She had a tank full
of water, so we could drink, wash and wash our clothes.
She fed us each day – and there were more than twenty
of us – and we rested there for a whole week. We
praised God together day after day, until eventually
we felt refreshed and strengthened and able to carry
on. A few days after we left, she fled too, and she's
now here in the camp with us.'

As Emeralde talked there were several nods and
murmurs of understanding and agreement. The only
interruptions came as others joined us, shook hands
with everyone in turn, and hugged Jennifer and me,
and then we all squashed closer together on the
benches. Etienne continued their story.

'The most frightening things were the road blocks.

There were dozens of them, every few hundred metres along the road. Each time we had to show our ID cards. If the militia decided someone was not to pass, they were told to stand to the side. Sometimes they were left to stand there for hours in the roasting sun, and then allowed to carry on. But sometimes the militia just waited till there was a group of them, and then they killed them all.

'There was one road block we came to which was particularly bad. There were soldiers as well, and they wouldn't let us pass. They told us we would have to wait till the next day. There was nothing we could do. No one would dare to disagree, so we sent the children off to find water and prepared to stay the night. They were away for ages, and it was getting dark. We were really worried about them, especially when the soldiers then began to move people on again. Eventually they came back, and we only had time for a quick drink – and the water was very dirty.

'When it was our turn at the road block they asked us for our papers, so we showed our ID cards as usual. But they began to get angry with us and said, "not these". I realised they were wanting money. They held a gun to my head, but I had no money left. They would have killed me, but then Emeralde remembered that she still had one 100 franc note [about 45 pence] left tied into her clothes. She gave it to the soldier and he was so happy that he let us go through. The Lord had protected us once again.'

As Etienne and Emeralde had been in the middle of speaking, Sarah, a friend from Gahini who had come in earlier, reached into a tattered blue plastic bag she had been clutching and brought out a Bible and hymn book.

When Etienne paused, she seized the opportunity to speak:

'If I may be allowed to take this opportunity, I would like to read you a Psalm, and I think we should sing hymn 196. But first I would like to tell you how the Lord looked after me, because I was stopped at one of those road blocks too. I showed my ID card, but the man snatched it out of my hand and said it couldn't be mine because it said Hutu, and he said I looked like a Tutsi. I told him that I was indeed a Hutu, and that what they were doing was very wrong. That God would judge them for this.'

I was amazed. I knew Sarah to be an unusually forthright and outspoken lady, but none the less it must have taken enormous courage to challenge the actions of these murderers when she knew she was at their mercy. She continued:

'He pushed me down to the verge at the side of the road, and I began to pray. I knew I was in God's hands, not theirs. At one point I looked up, and there were several men standing around me with their machetes raised ready to kill me. But as I watched, they lowered them and walked away. I'm sure there were angels protecting me. The man who had taken my ID card from me came and gave me it back and offered me an escort to walk with me. But I said to him, "I don't need your soldiers. Jesus will look after me."

'Now I would like to read you Psalm 23 because it is absolutely true.' We listened silently while she read, and then she passed me her hymn book, open at hymn 196. I took one glance at the hymn and my eyes immediately filled with tears. This was a hymn that Emeralde and I had sung together on a number of occasions when struggling through difficult patches. I looked across to Emeralde. Her eyes were full of compassion. She knew the agonies we had faced then, as well as the pain and torment of recent months.

With a trembling voice, and through my tears, I translated the hymn for Jennifer, and then we sang it all together. It spoke simply of Jesus knowing what the future holds for us, and knowing what is best for us; and of our need to trust ourselves to him, both now and for the future. Here in the depravation and the insecurity of this refugee camp, facing a bleak and unknown future, that was exactly what this group of people were doing.

'We're not here because of the war,' Sarah had said. 'We are here because God wants to teach us something. This is God's school for us at this time. So many good and wonderful things are happening.' I remembered Grace's first letter to me back in June just after they had arrived in Tanzania. She too had talked of being in a 'school', and of the valuable lessons God was teaching them.

Never would they have chosen to be in such dire circumstances. They, like so many others, were victims of the evil influences within their country. And yet, unlike many others around them, they had not been totally overwhelmed. As Christian people they knew their lives were safe with God. Time after time in the past they had experienced his remarkable way of bringing blessing and good out of disaster. And now even here, their lives totally committed to him, they were able to look positively on what to most would be an intolerable situation.

Sarah could happily have talked on for the rest of the afternoon, but I wanted first to hear the continuation of Etienne's and Emeralde's story. Emeralde took up the story from when they reached the bridge at the border with Tanzania – the same bridge we had crossed only days before:

'The border was closed. The army was guarding the bridge and we could not get anywhere near it, so we waited. After a few days we began to hear rumours that the RPF was getting much nearer, and that the soldiers guarding the bridge had fled. Everyone began to move again towards the bridge, but there were so many of us, we had to stand around for hours and hours.

'Eventually we reached the other side, but we had only gone a little way up the hill when we looked back and saw that the RPF had arrived. It was awful. People were panicking and pushing each other to try and cross. So many of them fell down the banks and off the bridge into the river. We were some of the last to cross before the RPF arrived and closed the bridge again.'

I could feel the tears well up in my eyes. I was picturing the scene, having seen the remnants strewn down the bank only a few days previously. Had they been just a few minutes later, they might have been in the water too. How many times had they just missed death? I could hardly bear to think of it.

While they had been talking, Jennifer had gone out in search of food for everyone. It was now well into the afternoon. She returned soon after with two bags, one full of chapatis, the other with bananas. The food was shared around, together with a small bag of peanuts we had brought. There was one chapati left over – the one with an omelette inside it. So it was duly divided up between all nineteen people and, after praising God for the good food, they tucked in.

While they were eating, I took the chance to ask a question. 'You know, we have been praying for you all these months, and we will continue to do so. But it would help us a lot to hear from you yourselves what you feel are the important things we should be praying for. What would *you* like us to pray for?' I was thinking of such things as peace, unity, security, for people to repent and turn to the Lord for forgiveness. The needs were many.

Grace was the first to reply, without a moment's hesitation. 'It's nearly the end of the year, and we don't know where we will get our Bible reading notes for next year. We have no money to buy them. Please will you ask people to pray that we can get our Scripture Union Bible reading notes.'

I could hardly believe it. Here was Grace, rejected by her family, barely surviving on her meagre one person's ration (having refused to say she was married with five children, as many single people did in order to get more food – 'That would be a lie, and the Bible teaches us not to lie' she had written to me). Here she was, hungry instead for the word of God, acknowledging its all importance in her life.

As it happened, just before leaving for Rwanda I had spoken with the British couple involved in the writing of these notes. They had told me that they were now being printed in Kenya, and would be distributed in the camps free of charge in the New Year! So her prayer had been answered already. That news brought a spontaneous cheer and clapping throughout the group and a rousing chorus of 'Yes, ashimwe' ('Praise Jesus'). After the meal most of the group left to allow me some time alone with Emeralde. Reluctantly, I too had to leave at four o'clock because of security regulations.

The following morning we were again delayed as various team members had mounds of urgent paperwork to complete before heading towards the camp. It was as we dropped in at another NGO compound that the news came through of a sudden deterioration in security in Goma camp, Zaire, across the north-western border of Rwanda. All NGO staff had apparently been pulled out.

This was bad news. Jennifer had been planning to travel there after leaving me back in Rwanda, to visit the Tear Fund/Christian Outreach Alliance team there, but perhaps it would not now be possible. We spent some time trying to radio and fax messages to seek clarification on the situation.

At the same time we were trying to find some form of transport back into Rwanda for the following day. We had just discovered that the flights that had been arranged from the UK a whole month previously did not exist! I was beginning to get a taste of the frustrations under which the team members had to operate. Last-minute changes in arrangements over which they had no control, lack of sufficient transport, cramped living and working conditions, and a deteriorating security situation within the camps – all these contributed to the high level of stress and tension which at times felt almost unbearable.

This was our last day in the camps. I had spent time with many people, but could not face going home without seeing Jeanne. Yet she was too weak to come to me, and initially I was too afraid to walk down into the camp to see her. However, the area where she lived was not the most densely populated, and therefore perhaps less risky for me. So with encouragement from my Rwandan parents, who seemed to have a finger on the pulse of the camp, Jennifer and I set off down the hill on foot.

It was, of course, the area where most of the folk from Gahini lived, so I recognised, and was recognised by, many people. Whether there were some who watched from a distance and refused to come and greet me, I will never know. But those who did come were many – hospital staff, young people from the local secondary school where Charles had been a teacher, little children and their mothers from the community around Gahini. A skinny, ragged child with a cheeky grin was pushed in front of me.

'Don't you remember her?' a woman asked me laughing. 'That's Sachet.'

I looked again at the child. Of course – I could never forget her and her sister with their hilarious names. She was one of seven children whom Anatolie and I had visited several times. The father was not known, and the family was extremely poor. Sachet (which is French for plastic or paper bag) often used to come and visit us in our office, together with her sister, Emballage (which is French for wrapping).

'Her mother was killed, you know. I have her now,' the woman said. I bent down and picked Sachet up, to the delight of those standing by. Outwardly she looked just the same as she always had done – grubby, torn clothes and skinny, but with a smiling face. Yet now she was an orphan, alone. What kind of future did this child face?

We walked on, surrounded by an ever-growing crowd, jostling and laughing around us. Suddenly my heart missed a beat. Approaching us was an elderly gentleman I knew from Gahini, whom I had been informed was one of the ringleaders of the killings there. He shuffled towards us, bent over a stick, and held out his hand to me. I took his hand and returned his greeting, looking straight at him. His stare, though, was fixed on the ground. He did not even lift his head, but turned and shuffled away again.

What was in his mind? What thoughts, what feelings, what agonies? His whole body seemed slumped in despair and hopelessness. And what hope was there for him? Without the love and forgiveness of Jesus, and the chance of a new life, there was nothing left to live for.

Eventually we reached Granny's house – a flimsy wooden frame about 6 feet by 12 feet, held together by bright-blue plastic. She pulled aside the piece of tattered cloth that hung over the doorway, which kept out the sun and prying eyes, and I bent down to follow her through.

Jeanne was lying on a thin mattress on the floor, covered by a sheet and a *kanga*. Her face was gaunt and pale, and she did not even lift her head as we came in. I knelt down beside her on the plastic floor, put my arm around her shoulders and my cheek to hers, and hugged her. Dear Jeanne, whom I thought I would never see again, but whose life God had amazingly spared even in the most dire of circumstances. She looked now as though she would not live to see tomorrow.

Jeanne reached for a hankie and tried to speak through her tears, but the words were hardly audible. 'I thought I would never see you again,' she whispered. One arm was bent under her head, and with the other she pushed the *kanga* off her body to reveal her mottled and scratched legs and stomach.

'You see this? My skin is so itchy and sore. It's horrible, but I have no cream to put on it. I just lie here all day and all night. I can't sleep, I'm so uncomfortable.

I can't eat that hard corn and beans – they hurt my mouth. Look.' She stuck out her tongue. It was covered with a thick white fur: thrush. I had met many people with AIDS in the course of my work in Gahini. It is such a horrible disease, but to see its devastating effect on one so close to me was almost too much.

For Jeanne, though, even worse than the physical symptoms was the guilt. 'It's my fault that we're here. We shouldn't have come. Mum did not want to come, but I insisted. I told her that for the sake of the children, we had to go. It's all my fault. Now I wish we were back in Rwanda. I miss the bananas, I miss our home, I miss the fields. We should never have come. And now I'll never go back to Rwanda.' Jeanne broke down into floods of tears.

'I've never told anyone that before,' Jeanne continued softly after a few moments. 'They have enough to cope with, without all my troubles.'

Jennifer and I listened as she poured out her heart, until gradually she began to calm down again. Then we talked together of all that she had done for the family, her hard work, her care, of things that were good. We talked of Jesus' forgiveness of things that had gone wrong, and of the beauty of heaven to come. And finally we prayed together. As we left Jeanne, there were no more tears. She even managed a smile as she promised to look out for us in heaven.

We had gone to the market that morning before coming into the camp, so she now had some fresh fruit and vegetables, some tea, sugar, powdered milk and fresh eggs (she liked to swallow them raw!), and some cream for her skin. At least for the last few days of her life she would have a little comfort.

It was soon after I returned to the UK that I received

a letter from Granny in which she told me of a remarkable improvement in Jeanne's health. She had regained so much strength that she had even been able to do some digging around their little house. However, just before Christmas 1994, she left behind her broken down body and is now in heaven with the Lord.

What a privilege. That was the first thought on my mind as we walked back up the hill to catch a lift back to Rwanda. What a privilege to be here, to spend time with these wonderful people, to share in their most intimate hopes and fears.

If only I could have stayed on with them. The world seemed such an unfair place. We had shared our homes and our lives together in Rwanda, but now I was going back to the comfort and security of the West, while they remained here in the harshness and poverty of the refugee camp. And yet among these Christian friends and family with whom I had spent the last few days, I had seen a depth of peace and a richness of faith that I had very rarely seen among the comfortable, materialistic Christians of the West.

As we approached the compound I could see the vehicle that was to take us back to Rwanda, and the group we were to be travelling with was already waiting for us. Yet there was one more thing I needed to do before leaving.

I had collected together a bag full of goodies for Grace – fruit, tea, skin cream and other things, but I knew it would not last for long. I wanted to leave her a more ongoing form of support. Grace had never once asked me for help; she never expected that just because I was white and rich that I could solve all her problems for her. Perhaps partly because of that, I even more wanted to do all I could to make life a little more bearable for her.

I had learned only the previous day that the Alliance needed a cook to prepare lunches each day for their small team. Surely Grace would be ideal for the job? This was a job she had done competently for years, and enjoyed. She was hard working and totally trustworthy; they could not ask for anyone better. And from Grace's point of view, it would not only provide her with a regular income, but she would be among Christian people; and because these were people I knew, it would be easy for us to keep in contact. That morning the Alliance team had agreed to employ her, so it was now up to me to pass on the good news.

The four people we were to travel with in the jeep were impatient to get away; there was no time for poignant goodbyes. As I told Grace of her new job, her face lit up in amazement. 'But I don't speak English – how will I manage?' she asked anxiously.

'You can teach them to speak Kinyarwanda instead. Don't worry, Paul and Laura will look after you,' I reassured her.

We wrapped our arms around each other for a brief poignant moment, then reluctantly Jennifer and I bundled into the back of the vehicle and it roared off. Grace stood between Paul and Laura, each with an arm around her, one hand holding a hankie to her face, the other waving. I watched and waved until they disappeared out of sight, and still the tears streamed silently down my dusty face.

'Would you like some chocolate, or a cookie?' came the strong American drawl. 'Oh don't worry, we've got plenty here.'

9

Gahini Revisited

When I first went to Rwanda I used to travel regularly on public transport. The clapped-out old minibuses, otherwise known as taxis, ran reasonably frequently and were very cheap. It could be a pretty uncomfortable ride, squashed into a sixteen-seater bus with twenty-five to thirty people (to say nothing of their luggage, chickens, sacks of grain, etc.), lurching round corners and screeching to a halt to pick up yet more passengers. The only alternative would have been to hire our project vehicle, but the taxis were very much cheaper.

Now, after the war, it was an encouraging sign to see these taxis on the road again, and to know that people were once again travelling around the countryside.

Two weeks previously, when I had first gone back to Gahini, I had promised Beatrice and some of the nurses that I would take a taxi out to visit them again and stay for a few days. However, my visit to the refugee camp had quickly changed that idea. The heightened tensions and the rumours of imminent attacks made me realise that the situation was still far from stable. If there were to be an invasion from the camps into Rwanda, the taxis would stop immediately and I would be totally stranded. So I knew I had to find some alternative, safer means of getting to Gahini.

There were 134 NGOs working in Rwanda, most of them based in the capital, Kigali, but with projects around the country. One of these had set up an orphanage south of Gahini. I discovered that three of their Kigali-based Rwandan staff were due to make a visit there soon, and would be happy to drop me off in Gahini and then collect me in the afternoon. It was the perfect solution.

It was already late morning by the time we reached Gahini. Samweli, the driver, stopped outside the church and I jumped out.

'See you back here around two o'clock then,' he said.

'Two? I'll believe that when I see it,' I laughed. 'You'll not make it back here by then, but I'll try and be ready anyway – see you.'

I walked past the church and along the road behind the hospital, carefully avoiding the water-logged potholes.

My first stop was Rusi's little house. A single, elderly lady who hobbled about on crutches because she had only one leg, Rusi spent much of her time in her tiny crumbling bedroom, praying. She had become a Christian during the East Africa revival of the 1930s, through the love and care of the Christian staff in Gahini Hospital. Now, in response, she spent many hours a day alone in her little house, praying for the staff and the hospital.

I picked my way through the overgrown banana patch, round to the back of the house. I called 'hello', but there was no response, so I pushed open the rickety old wooden door, bent down to avoid knocking my head on the low frame, and stepped inside. In the darkness I could not tell who or what was in the room, but by the strong smells I sensed there must be a chicken or two, and some scraps of food that were older than yesterday's abandoned on the uneven earthy floor.

Rusi recognised my voice immediately. As I ducked through the doorway into her tiny bedroom, she was already sitting up on the edge of her bed, hands held up to her face in amazement. Without a word, I bent down to greet her with a hug. For a few seconds we clasped each other tightly in silence, then she could hold back no longer.

'Iman' ishimwe! Iman' ishimwe! Iman' ishimwe!' ['Praise God! Praise God! Praise God!'] she exclaimed, patting me on the back again and again. Her deep joy and gratitude in being remembered and visited overflowed in praise to God, the One who had sustained her all these years and protected her through the horrors of the past months.

I sat on the edge of the bed beside her as she grasped my hands tightly in hers and related to me God's goodness in the midst of all the tragedies. She was close to tears as she reflected on the evil actions of those known to us both, those who took part in the massacres.

'May the Lord forgive them for what they have done,' she said. 'Lord, forgive all of us Rwandans for rejecting you.'

Her body was weak and frail, but her spirit was undauntable; she was an inspiration to be with. She was delighted to have someone to talk to, and would happily have chatted all day. However, I still had others I wanted to see, so after a little while I excused myself, promising to try to return later in the day.

By this time, word had somehow spread that I was back in Gahini, and as I left Rusi's house I was met by some children who had been sent to fetch me. I followed them along the paths, between the houses, until we reached Gahini's commercial centre. 'Out the back' we used to call it, for want of a better description. It was the local centre of activity. In the daytime a few small shops sold an amazing selection of essential items, everything from sardines to soap, from clothes to kettles, from tomato puree to torches. A couple of mud houses doubled up as restaurants, the newly slaughtered goat hanging up outside the door, exposed to the sun, flies and dust. Women spread their wares out on the ground at the side of the road – a row of neat piles of tomatoes, a few cabbages, a basket full of bunches of bananas.

In the evenings, after sunset at six-thirty, the scene changed. The shops became drinking dens, overflowing with groups of men noisily passing round gourds of the potent local brew. Prostitution was rife here.

I approached the little T junction in the centre and looked around me. It was as if nothing had changed; business was carrying on as usual. Shops were open, goat kebabs sizzled on the open fires, people stood around chatting. But there was one stark difference. I recognised no one, and no one recognised me. These people were all newcomers. Some had fled into Gahini in search of security, abandoning their isolated homes in the countryside. Others were returnees to Rwanda, delighted to be home after thirty-five years in exile. They had simply moved in and taken over vacant homes and businesses, abandoned back in April and May 1994.

I tried to take it all in, this Gahini that I had known, now under new management. In some ways, life for me had stood still for the past six months; it was as if I had only left a week ago. Subconsciously I half expected everything to be as it was before, but it could never be. Yet I began to realise that for the people here, life carried on. Six months was a long time: enough time to set up home; time to plant crops. Yes, time even to establish a community.

However, it was a community to which I no longer belonged, and I felt strange. Even as I paused to look around me, there was a sort of emptiness, a hollowness inside me. Yet again it hit me – this enormous grief I was living through. The loss of so much that had made up my life.

The children went ahead of me into one of the shops, and a shiver went up my spine as I followed them. Something suddenly reminded me of one the locals I used to bump into in this shop. He had been a friend of ours – or so I had thought – and a respected member of the community. Yet when the killing began, according to several people I had spoken to, he was one of the ring-leaders responsible for the massacres in Gahini. Had Charles and I still been in Gahini when it began, would he have sanctioned our murder too?

I had realised long ago that we might well not have survived had we been in Gahini back in April, but to be killed by someone we had known well? It was almost inconceivable, and yet it was a pattern that had been repeated thousands of times all over the country. The killers *knew* their victims: they were their neighbours, their teachers, their students, their colleagues. Some of the men in the gang who had murdered Anatolie had lived only a few hundred yards from her home. My mind could scarcely take in such horrors, but the stories were the same, again and again.

It took a moment for my eyes to adjust from the

bright sunshine outside the dim light within the shop. There were three or four people standing around inside, but the lady standing laughing behind the counter attracted my attention immediately. It was Joelle, an old friend of ours.

'So you survived too!' I exclaimed with delight. I was amazed that this Tutsi lady, with relatives in the RPF, should have managed to escape the massacres. She continued to laugh as she clapped me on the back in a warm embrace.

'You've come back,' she said. 'You've come back home again to help us. You're here to stay, aren't you?' It was not so much a question as an assumption.

I tried to pass over the comment by mumbling something about being on a visit, and perhaps coming back later. However, it was not easy; once again I felt torn. For a brief moment I began again to question myself. Could I cope with coming back after all that had happened? Would it be safe for me? Now, though, was not the time to think about these big questions.

Joelle was the only one behind the counter. Was she in charge of the shop now, I wondered. Perhaps like so many others, in the absence of the rightful owner, she had seized the opportunity to run a profitable business, and had simply moved in and taken over. Yet before I had a chance as ask her, she began to relate to me what had happened to her back in April. Joelle described how she had fled to Rukara, the local administrative centre some twelve kilometres away, and sought refuge in the large Catholic church.

My stomach lurched. I knew Rukara Catholic church well, and had been horrified to see it on the television back in May. It had been the site of a terrible massacre in which thousands had been killed. I had seen the piles of mutilated bodies lying between the wooden benches, blood streaked all down the walls. So Joelle had been in that awful place but had *survived*. I would not have imagined it possible.

But it was possible. The militia had been unable to break down the doors, so instead they had thrown grenades through the windows. Day after day people were blown up all around her, suffering unbelievable agony and death. My head reeled as she described it all. It was so horrendous that it seemed unreal. I did not ask how many days they suffered such torture inside that death hole, but eventually the RPF reached the area and the few who were still alive were able to leave in safety.

I was profoundly moved by Joelle's courage, and amazed at her seeming absence of bitterness, as she related her experiences to me, despite all she had been through. I wondered if I would not have cracked up completely under the same circumstances. But Joelle was a Christian, and deeply aware that it was not her own strength and resources that had sustained her.

The conversation then moved on to other things, news of the family and others I had known. People came and went in the shop. I was listening, but what I heard remained perched on the surface of my mind. Deep down I was so completely numbed that I could not take in any more.

My time in Gahini was rushing by, and I was conscious that I had other business to see to before returning to Kigali. So once more I excused myself, promising to try and pop in again before leaving.

Since our first return visit to Gahini some two weeks previously, I had gleaned some interesting information through various conversations. Despite our pleas on that first visit, Jennifer and I had been refused permission to go near the house that Charles and I had lived in as it was ostensibly in a military zone. It turned out, however, that the very soldier who had denied us access was himself living in our house!

It might be possible, I thought to myself, to find some excuse to visit him, so I could see our old house just once more. I then had an idea.

Before setting off for Rwanda in September, we had contacted the RPF to explain our reason for travel. In response they sent us official papers promising us assistance in our search for Charles. During our previous visit to Gahini, when the request to visit our house was refused, I had left these papers with the soldier. He in turn had promised to contact his seniors in Kigali and try to obtain permission for us to visit the house.

At least, this is what he had said at the time. I now realised it was probably just a stalling technique, a means to get rid of us. Surely this man had the right to receive visitors in his own house without contacting his seniors in Kigali! Yet it was worth a follow-up visit. I could ask him whether his discussions with his seniors had been successful.

It was now after one o'clock in the afternoon. Lunchtime – the ideal time to visit. So having first checked to make sure that he was not in his office, I began to make my way towards our old home.

I forgot, of course, that you can never go anywhere in Africa in a hurry! There were so many people on the road – people I had not seen for six months. Each wanted to talk to me, to tell me what had happened to them.

'Rezire! Please come inside. My wife is here too. Did you know that she survived too? Come and eat with us.' One of our male nurses led me into what had now become his house, its previous occupants having fled to Tanzania.

I hugged his wife, while the children in turn threw their arms around me. It would have been rude to leave immediately, so I sat with them for a few minutes. Yet I was anxious to get on and reach my house before two o'clock, before the soldier returned to work.

But I did not get much farther along the road. Coming running towards me, arms outstretched, his broad grin revealing two missing front teeth, was the youngest son of our good friends, Simon and Christine. 'Mama, ni Rezire! Mama ni Rezire!' ['Mum, it's Lesley!'] he cried out in delight, wrapping his arms firmly around my thighs, his head buried in my skirt.

This young couple and their four children had lived very near to us before the war. Once again, I had feared the worst for them. Both parents and children were tall, slim and fine-featured – what many would have described as typical Tutsis and therefore an obvious target for the militia. Yet somehow they had survived. How lovely it was to see them again!

I could not refuse their invitation to go in and share a cup of black tea with them. (Milk and sugar were now unaffordable luxuries.) Their own lovely house had been taken over, so they had moved into another one that was vacant. Its previous owners had also fled to Tanzania.

It was dark and dingy inside. The walls, previously whitewashed, were now covered with dirty hand and finger prints that could not be washed off; dozens of people had sheltered here, as in most other substantial

homes, after the RPF took over Gahini. These people
had been too afraid to leave the security of the military
refugee camp and return to their homes in the hills
where the militia were still at large.

But what of Simon and Christine? How on earth did
they manage to escape?

'We were sure we would all be killed,' Christine
began. 'But we thought, if only just one of our children
could survive, then at least the whole family would not
be wiped out. I sent a message with our worker up to
your house to ask if you would protect one of our boys.
But he came back and told us that you were not there,
that you had gone to Kenya. Our hearts sank then, for
we knew we couldn't stay in the house for long or they
would find us and kill us. Yet it was far too dangerous
to go out. In the end we decided to try to cross the lake
to Mukarange, because we had heard the killing had
not really reached there. We had a Hutu friend with a
boat who agreed to take us across by night.'

'But would that not have been very dangerous for
him?' I asked.

'Oh yes. If he had been caught he would definitely
have been killed for helping us. But he was a good
man, and we knew we could trust him. When we got
there we didn't know anyone, but we asked a family if
we could hide with them. They took us in and we
stayed there for a couple of days. It was a lot safer than
Gahini, because neighbours weren't turning on each
other. But then the militia came from farther along the
lake and the killing started there too. So we all fled out
into the bushes not far from the house.'

I knew the area a little. It was less densely populated
than Gahini, so there were more scrubby areas of trees
and bushes to hide in.

'We hid there for a day and a night without any food or water. I was sure we were all going to die, but it got even worse. Sometimes we could see and hear the militia hunting people down. They were chopping down the bushes and long grass with their machetes, and then attacking the people they found. They were like dogs hunting down a wild animal. That's how they thought of us – just wild animals to be hunted down and killed.'

There was a tremor in Christine's voice. It was clearly still very distressing for her to remember what she had lived through. Tears trickled down my cheeks and I shook my head in disbelief. Tears of distress for all they had suffered. Tears of anger that anyone should treat human life so cheaply. Tears of relief that, although I had not been there to help them as they had wished, none the less God had been merciful to this family and spared them.

Christine continued their story:

'We began to think logically about the situation and decided that if we were to be killed, we might as well be inside a house with food and water as out in the open exposed to the mosquitoes and the cold at night. So we went back to the house where we had been.

'The next day the militia came to the house and asked if we were the owners. When we told them that we were visitors and that the owners had fled, they went away again. It was an absolute miracle! And they didn't come back again! It wasn't long after that we heard the RPF had taken Gahini, so we went back. God spared not just one of us, but all of us. It really is a miracle! We thank God every day that we're all still alive.'

They both lost a lot of weight and were looking very gaunt, despite having been back in Gahini for nearly six months. Christine had resumed her teaching job at the local primary school, but had not yet been paid. They had no fields for growing their own food, so they were dependent on hand-outs distributed to all the refugees in the Gahini area.

Previously they had both had good jobs, a nice house and healthy, well-dressed children. Now they looked like the poor people from out in the countryside; life must be so tough for them. Yet there was still a dignity and poise about Christine. She would always be a gracious lady, no matter the difficulty of their circumstances.

'But what about you, Lesley?' she asked. 'What news have you of Charles? We've been so concerned for you.'

There was such genuine care in her voice that I almost burst into tears. During these weeks that I had been in Rwanda I had had little time to face my own tragedy. Everyone I spoke to had their own tale to tell; each poured out their story to me, one after another. It was not that I did not want to listen to them, but it meant that I had to shelve my own feelings, time after time. In many ways, my sadness seemed so minor compared to theirs. 'Huh, you're lucky,' was the reply on more than one occasion when I mentioned that Charles was missing and rumoured dead. 'You've only lost one. I've lost thirty members of my family.' Or maybe it was fifty, or even a hundred.

I explained to Christine what little I knew, the rumours that had reached me from various sources, but that had not been confirmed. Deep inside, I had still been holding out hope of Charles turning up eventually, but I was now slowly beginning to realise that the chances were very slim.

Christine was silent for a few moments. There had been a deep bond of trust and friendship between them and Charles ever since he had come to Gahini in 1991. It was so painful for them to hear this news.

As we talked there was a knock at the door. Someone had come to see them. I glanced at my watch – it was gone two o'clock! I was supposed to be at the house before two. I wished I could have stayed for longer. There was so much more to talk over, and many questions I wanted to ask, but my time in Gahini was running out.

I walked quickly round the side of the large red-brick church, and started down the hill. The beauty of the place struck me once again. Huge old trees, heavy with blossom, lined the road from the church, giving an air of permanence and stability. And yet now there was neither permanence nor stability. So much had changed from how it had been, and the future was very uncertain. It was all so familiar, and yet all completely different.

I slowed down as I reached the point where the road forked – the right led past the old rehabilitation centre, and towards the front of the hospital; straight on led down the hill to the main road. Which path should I take to my house? The front way to the right? No, it's too obvious, I thought to myself. I'll go round the back paths where I'm less likely to be seen.

I felt uneasy, half expecting to be stopped at any moment by soldiers whom I assumed would be guarding the house. However, there was no one to be seen as I approached the house. To my amazement, the old shabby gates to the driveway were hanging wide open, and there were no soldiers guarding it.

So I walked straight through, my mind only half taking in where I was, the other half whirring round and round with the morning's conversations. I had reached the front of the house before I was spotted. Two young lads over on the grass by the side door had been too busily engrossed in their task of washing clothes to notice my approach. By the time one had sprinted across and leapt on to the balcony in front of me, I was already walking up the steps.

Through the open door I could see immediately the reason why my presence was not desired there. Far from the house having been 'totally looted and emptied', as I had been told by the soldier on my previous visit, I found myself looking straight at our own settee and armchairs. Hanging on the wall behind was one of our locally painted pictures, and a wood carving we had received for a wedding present. It was almost as I had left it six months previously. I could not believe my eyes.

I had not expected this; it threw me completely. Yet somehow I managed to retain some composure while negotiating with the young lad for permission to wait for the occupier. Having got this far, I had no intention of leaving straight away.

Eventually, with the arrival of some other visitors by car, the soldier to whom we had spoken on our first visit appeared from inside. It was true then; he was indeed the occupier of our house.

The half-hour that followed must have been one of the most horrible of my life. This time I was conscious only of my own desperate situation: my husband had most probably been murdered; I had lost my job, home and possessions; many friends had been killed. I had been struggling for the last six months to come to terms with what felt like the total collapse of my whole life.

Inside the house, with my back to the bookshelf, I was just able to see through a gap in the ragged piece of curtain, draped across the wide archway between the sitting-room, where we were, and the dining-room. I was surprised to see our long, low dining-room cabinet, seemingly intact and in its usual place. Perhaps the rest of our embroidered cloths and placemats were still in the drawers, and the dishes, cutlery and glasses still in the cupboards, I thought. In fact, perhaps that means there may still be many personal things in our bedroom too.

A few African crafts remained on the top shelf of the bookshelves – a traditional wooden milk jug with basket lid which had been one of the essential items of the ibirongoranwa (the-things-a-new-bride-brings-with-her-to-her-new-home); one beautifully carved impala book-end given to me by Lionel and Mary after I had delivered their second child in their home in Gahini; a couple of bright blue, hand-embroidered cloths made at Kiziguru, a nearby Catholic sewing project, now destroyed.

Suddenly these few remaining items took on a huge significance. They were a tangible link with a whole period of my life that had been wrenched out of my hands. It now seemed desperately important to me that I should be able to take some things away with me – things which could never be replaced, which represented my life, my husband, my home, my friends.

At that moment I had no thoughts for the circumstances of the soldier sitting in front of me. It did not occur to me that he had probably lost dozens of his family members; that perhaps he was back in his homeland for the first time in his life, having been brought up as a refugee abroad when his parents fled earlier massacres. It did not cross my mind how much he too must have suffered, or how he must have felt arriving in Gahini with no home or possession to call his own. Was it any wonder he did not want me back?

I asked him if I might take a few small items with me. 'No, this is not your house,' he replied. 'Nothing in here belongs to you. You have no right to be here, and I had told you that you were not to come.' His voice was calm and he spoke softly, but with a cold authority.

The discussion between us then became heated and tense, until suddenly I realised I could go no further. I was now the visitor; he was the occupier. I was a Westerner, no longer belonging to Rwanda; but Rwanda was now his home. He was a military man, to be feared and obeyed; I was a nobody. The balance was very firmly tipped in his direction. But more than that. I also realised that he was a powerful man, and that I had posed a threat to him, however insignificant. What was there to stop him silencing me – once and for all?

It was with a fearful, heavy and angry heart that I said goodbye, walked out of the front door of our house and slowly back up the garden path. Forbidden to take with me even one small object, I left behind me all that linked me with the past, with Charles and with a whole era of my life.

The gate seemed a long way away. I was sure this would be the last time I would ever walk this path. If I survived today, I could certainly never come back here again, for fear of my life. I had been home, I had sat again where Charles and I had sat together so many times. For a few moments I had stepped back in history.

But now it was gone; lost for ever. I was walking away from a life that never would be again, and with nothing but memories to hold on to.

I walked through the shabby tin gates and paused. Safe – at least I was safe.

I had my life. That was all.

10

Isla

I stumbled bewildered up the narrow earthy path that led from our house to the rough hospital road. I was just managing to hold back the tears, but knew they would come pouring out at the first opportunity, and I desperately felt the need to talk to someone. I could not face going back up to the hospital in such a state. I felt it wouldn't be fair to land myself on my friends there; they had enough of their own problems to deal with – much worse than mine.

So instead of following the road round to the right, up towards the bright-blue hospital gates, I continued straight on. I walked slowly along the short stretch of road that connected the houses of the few British hospital staff. On my left, behind the hedge and down beyond the large grassy area, was a long low white-washed house. It had been Rob's and Trisha's home.

I stood for a few moments, my mind shifting between total blank numbness and whirling with a thousand and one memories all coming at once. Suddenly I realised there was someone approaching; it was a young girl.

'Where are you going?' she asked me.

I evaded her question, not knowing the answer myself. Instead, I asked her a question.

'Who lives in that house?' I pointed with my chin towards Rob's and Trisha's old home.

'That's the *Bourgemeistre's* house.'

'And that one?' I continued, referring to the next house in the row, a substantial solid-brick building with a rusty tin roof. It had been the home of one of the physiotherapists, Liz, for the past twenty-three years.

'The doctor lives there – that Rwandan lady who came from Rwamagana,' she replied.

Neither Rob and Trisha nor Liz had been back into Rwanda since they had had to flee in early April when their own lives were threatened. Like me, they had been told that their houses had been looted, so I knew they would be very keen for me to gather any information I could. This was not the moment, though, to make enquiries.

I reached the corner and started down the slope towards the garden of the house I lived in before I got married. What a mess! In the past it had been a neatly laid-out productive vegetable garden. We had grown all sorts of produce – carrots, peppers, leeks, cabbages, tomatoes, onions, rhubarb, aubergines, and many more. Each bed had been neatly edged with bamboo canes, and there had hardly been a weed in sight. Now it was barely recognisable.

As I reached the house there was no one in sight, so I walked through under the car port to the front balcony. It was three houses really, all joined together. Mine had been the far one. I could not see it from where I stood, as it was set back just a little.

However, I could see the middle house clearly. During the political tensions of the past years, I had always assumed that someone living in one of these houses would be safe. They had solid metal doors front and back, and thick iron bars over the windows, cemented into the wall. In the frenzied killings of April and May, though, these houses had offered no protection. The iron bars over one window had been completely ripped out and the metal window frame forced off the wall. A large hole was left, big enough for any number of killers to enter the house and slaughter the helpless victims who had sought refuge inside. A chill ran through me as I wondered who it might have been.

I looked inside. The walls were covered in reddish-brown finger marks and streaks. There was one single piece of furniture, a long low cupboard, presumably too solid and heavy to carry away when the rest of the furniture was looted.

I stood for a few moments, wondering if I dare take some pictures. There was no sign of life anywhere, so I took out my camera. Predictably, just at that moment a figure appeared. A young Rwandan nun, with a dark-blue habit, white head covering and a smiling face, came towards me. I quickly stuffed my camera back in my bag.

I explained briefly why I was there, and she listened sympathetically. Perhaps she could see my distress, despite my trying so hard to remain composed. She took my arm and led me along the balcony of the middle house, towards my own. Her kindness was too much for me, contrasting so vividly with what I had just been through with the soldier. At the first sight of my former house, I had to turn away. I tried to hide the tears that were beginning to roll uncontrollably down my cheeks.

Two other nuns came out of this house to greet me, one elderly, the other very young. I assumed they were now living in my former house. They brought me hot sweet tea, bananas, and a plate of UN high-protein biscuits. As we talked, I learned that they had fled to Gahini themselves at the beginning of the war and had not yet been able to go back to their own homes in southern Rwanda. They also had living with them a young boy of about ten and a girl of about seventeen. The boy had been brought to Gahini Hospital for treatment for a heart condition. He had made a good recovery, but had no home to go to. *All* of his family had been killed in the war. He was totally alone, apart from the nuns. The girl too was alone – some of her family had been killed, and the rest had fled.

The nuns told me that they were expecting to be moved on to a different location within the next few days, so the children would be left on their own to survive as best they could.

As we sat on the balcony talking, looking at the overgrown hillside across the valley, a stray dog bounded through the hedge into the garden. It was dark brown and lean-looking. The young boy chased it away. I did not recognise it, but I immediately thought of Isla, my own dog, which I had left behind six months ago. I had been told she had been killed, but needed to be sure.

'You haven't by any chance seen a light-coloured dog around here – about the colour of that biscuit?' I asked half-heartedly, pointing to the UN biscuits.

'Well yes, actually,' the smiling nun replied. 'There has been a dog hanging around here a bit. She had puppies behind that hedge there, but I haven't seen her for a while.'

My heart missed a beat. Isla would be likely to come back here if she was having puppies; it was a familiar, safe place to her. Maybe she was still alive after all! I wanted to get up immediately to go and look, but I had not finished my tea and felt it would be rude to leave in the middle – especially because of a dog!

I swallowed the last few mouthfuls, declined a refill, and suggested we go to have a look. One of the nuns came with me. We walked along the balcony, dodging the trailing honeysuckle, and round the side of the house. To the left of the narrow passageway were sheds, the red-brick water storage system, and the outside 'long drop' with its bright-red wooden door.

I followed the nun as she climbed up the couple of brick steps on to the small wall that had separated Lionel's and Mary's house from mine. It was difficult to tell where the gap in the hedge had been; the whole hedge had now collapsed.

Sloping down to our left had been their vegetable garden. I had used it too, after Lionel and Mary had left. A brick path down the middle led to a mud hut with a grass roof, right at the bottom of the garden. Lionel had built this as a 'prayer hut' – a place to go for quiet and peace, to be alone with God, or to meet with others for prayer. I looked at where it had been. A mound of earth was in its place; there was no brick path left. In fact, the whole garden was upturned, just uneven piles of earth and weeds.

I picked my way carefully over the clods. There was something extremely unpleasant about this garden now. The nun caught my arm and leaned over to me. 'There are many bodies buried here,' she whispered, indicating the garden around us.

I froze on the spot. Without daring to move another step, I looked more closely at the ground around me. Of course, that was it. These were not just mounds of earth all around me. There were bones sticking out of the earth, bits of skulls, pieces of clothing. This was a mass grave. Our garden had been used as a mass grave, and I was walking in the middle of it. I felt very sick.

I had come face to face with the results of the genocide. This time it was not on the television; it was not in the newspaper; it was not just a picture. This was reality. This was what had actually happened. People had been hacked up in our very own garden and thrown into our vegetable plot. Perhaps I was actually walking on people that I knew.

I could hardly take it in. Never before had I been faced with such blatant evil. I could imagine the frenzy of the killers, wielding machetes, sticks, clubs, drunk with the desire to destroy. I could feel the terror of those who knew they were targets, nowhere to hide, no one to protect them. It was the same all over the country. I had heard it so many times before, but this time I felt it too. I looked at the pieces of mutilated bodies that remained.

How could this happen? Why did it happen? Why, O God, why? How dare anyone treat life so cheaply? What kind of madness had inspired them? Never before had I come face to face with the depths of evil to which people are capable of sinking. Now here it was before my very eyes. Evil at its worst; Satan unrestrained. Tears of anger and sorrow welled up and burned my eyes.

The nun was waiting for me down by the hedge at the bottom of the garden. I continued carefully, treading as gently as possibly, and caught up with her. We picked our way through the long dry grass and prickly bushes, peering under the hedge as we went.

'She was about here when I last saw here,' she said, pointing to a gap under the hedge. 'There's no sign of

her puppies now. She must have moved them somewhere else.'

I was not ready to give up so easily, and continued a
few more steps alongside the hedge. Suddenly a dog
darted out a few yards in front of me. It was just the
colour and size of Isla! It glanced back before running
away, but I was sure it was her. 'Isla! Isla! Come
here, pup!' She recognised my voice immediately and
turned to look at me. I called her again, and this time
there was no hesitation. I dropped my bag and camera
and fell to my knees as she came bounding towards
me, crying, squealing, yelping. She was all over me at
once, jumping, licking, whining, wriggling everywhere.
I did not care that she was filthy and covered in ticks.
Isla was alive! I could hold back the tears no longer.
They poured uncontrollably down my cheeks, and my
whole body was wracked with agony and grief as the
emotions of the past hours in Gahini at last found an
outlet.

'She's a lot skinnier now,' the nun said. 'She used to
be quite fat. All the wild dogs were fat.' I looked up
from the bumpy soil, and the nun saw the look of
puzzlement on my face. 'They were living off human
flesh, you see,' she explained. 'They ate the bodies left
rotting on the hillsides.'

Once again my stomach lurched. Isla, my pet dog,
eating *people*? *How could she*? My joy at finding her alive
turned immediately to disgust. Perhaps she had been
eating some of my friends? I could hardly bear to think
of it.

But then I realised I couldn't blame her. Dogs have
no sense of morality, only an instinct to survive at any
cost. She had been abandoned by me, frightened,
hungry. Was it any surprise that she had made use of

the only source of food around – the hundreds of
corpses strewn over the hills? It was yet another sickening consequence of a brutal and senseless genocide.

My joy at finding Isla was quickly replaced by deep
sorrow, for I knew I couldn't take her with me and that
the nuns themselves would soon be moving on. Oh
why did I have to find her? I thought to myself. It
would have been better to believe that she was dead,
as I had been told. Now I'm going to have to leave Isla,
abandon her again. Who knows what will happen to
her now? I felt so wretched. Everything had been
wrenched out of my hands – my husband, my friends,
our home and all our possessions. But now, the one
thing that was still there, the one remaining part of my
life, precious and familiar, I was leaving behind. It felt
too much to bear.

The vehicle was due to collect me at two o' clock. I
knew they would be late, perhaps several hours late,
but it was now well past the expected time. I ought to
go back to the hospital to see if they had arrived. The
nuns accompanied me back up the grassy path to the
road, and we said goodbye.

Yet Isla insisted on coming with me, trotting along
just behind me. We reached the edge of Lionel's and
Mary's hedge where the hospital came into view. From
here it was just 50 yards or so on the worn track to
reach the gates. I had walked this path hundreds of
times in the past, firmly insisting that Isla wait by the
hedge. The hospital was supposed to be out of bounds
to her, although she used to sneak in when I was out of
sight to scavenge for scraps of food.

We stopped by the hedge, and she looked at me
expectantly. How could I do this to her? I buried my

face in her soft ear and gave her a final cuddle. 'Isla, I'm sorry.' My tears dripped on to her tick-infested fur.

'Stay!' I said firmly, as I stood up and began to make my way towards the hospital. After a few steps I turned around again. Isla was still sitting in exactly the same place. Did she think I had only gone to work, that I'd be back again soon? I pointed my finger at her and repeated the command, 'Stay!' There was no need to – she was such a good dog; she just sat there obediently.

I reached the hospital gates and walked through. I could still see Isla beside the hedge, watching my every step. She watched until she could see me no more, as I passed between the buildings, with a final glance back – and a lump of lead in the pit of my stomach.

I sat quietly for most of the hour-long journey back to Kigali. The three Rwandans with me had been visiting an orphanage in Kibungo, and seemed to have a lot to discuss. My mind was far away as I stared out of the window. How could I tell them of the horrors I had heard and seen? It had long since become familiar to them. Nearly everyone had lost their homes and possessions – so what if I had too? And as for Isla, it would be totally incomprehensible to Rwandans to be so distressed over a dog.

My heart was in my boots as we bumped slowly down the rutted, muddy road from Gahini and turned on to the smooth tarmac alongside the lake. I wondered if I would ever go back. Probably not for a long time to come. I had endangered my life once, and got away with it, but perhaps I would not be so lucky the next time. The soldier in our old house would not forget me quickly. Fear began to grip me again as I realised how vulnerable I was, even in Kigali. It would not be difficult for him to follow my movements and arrange an 'accident' for me. I still had one week left in Rwanda.

I tried to put these thoughts out of my head and stared out of the window at the countryside flying past. The houses dotting the edge of the road and the hillside beyond showed little sign of life. Before the genocide the roads were always teeming with life, from first light around five o'clock in the morning until well past sunset at six-thirty in the evening. There used to be people everywhere: brightly dressed women heading to and from the market; men riding their heavily laden bicycles; girls in bright-blue dresses and boys in khaki shorts, running barefooted away from school, laughing and playing. I could almost see them – but they were no longer there.

In their place was an eerie quiet. Where houses had once stood, all that remained was a pile of crumbling mud bricks. Field upon field, where women had toiled laboriously, lay silent, the over-ripe crops now choked by weeds. Large sticks of green bananas hung down on the palms by the roadside, no one to gather them in.

'You're very quiet, Lesley. How have you got on today? How's Gahini?'

'I've had a bit of a rough day,' I replied, focusing my mind back on the people around me in the car. I would rather have left it at that, but Samweli was in a talkative mood. He wanted to know more.

'I went back to our house,' I continued. 'I suppose I shouldn't have really. There's a soldier living in it – and it's full of our stuff. He didn't like my coming – we had quite a heated conversation. When I think about it now, he could have killed me.'

'Why would he do that? You haven't done anything,'

he said. My thinking clearly did not make sense to Samweli.

'I wanted to take some of our things, and he absolutely refused. You see, I could make life difficult for him. I could expose his corruption. So really, it's in his interests to get rid of me. I've heard of other situations where someone coming back to claim their house has just "disappeared".'

Samweli laughed. 'That doesn't happen – it's just stories. There are proper procedures to follow to claim back property. You'll just have to be patient, but you'll get it back eventually.'

'So you don't think he'll try to track me down in Kigali then?' I asked anxiously.

'You don't need to worry,' he said. 'These guys have much more important things to do.'

It was not an issue for Samweli, but his assurances did little to alleviate my anxiety. Sometimes it was hard to know who to believe. Samweli was a Tutsi, as were most of the soldiers of the RPF. He sympathised with their need for accommodation and transport, which led to their appropriating other people's houses and vehicles. He was clearly at ease, and had confidence in them.

Hutu friends, on the other hand, were not quite so accommodating. Some of them were evidently very fearful of the soldiers, relating to me examples of mysterious disappearance and night-time killings.

Where did the truth lie? Who do I believe? Were they somehow both true? I used to ask Charles these kind of questions. I could always trust him to give me an honest answer – but he was no longer here.

On reaching Kigali, we turned sharply off the main road and on to a rough narrow street between two houses. It widened out as we continued down the side of the hill; the houses here were more close together than in the countryside, but each still had a small patch for growing beans and a few banana palms. There were noticeably more people around in the town.

A large metal entrance gate on our right was swinging off its hinges as we approached. I gasped as I looked inside. This had obviously been a beautiful house, solidly built, with a spacious, colourful garden. All that remained was a shell, a few tumbling walls and window frames, amid a massive pile of mangled metal and bricks.

The lady sitting beside me in the car saw me looking, and told me the name of the businessman who had lived there with his wife and family. We passed several more destroyed homes. She knew all the people who had lived in them – teachers, businessmen, drivers – mostly Tutsis. She too was a Tutsi, and this was not her home area. So how on earth had she survived, when so many others had been killed? We reached her home and stopped the car outside.

'Haven't you heard her story?' Samweli asked me. 'It's amazing. A real miracle from God.'

She stayed in the car and pulled the door shut again. There was silence as she began to speak.

The killings had begun in her area on the morning of 7 April, the day after the president's plane was shot down. From their house they could hear screams all around, as men, women and children were dragged from their homes and slaughtered. She knew that it was only a matter of time before the murderers reached their house. To stay would mean almost certain death. She had to try and find a safe place for her four children.

Quickly she ushered them out of the house, and through the back lanes. Yet once out on the streets it immediately became clear that no place would be safe. There were road blocks everywhere. The streets were swarming with young men, heads and faces partially covered, wielding machetes, knives, clubs with nails – even pointed umbrellas. Crowds stood around every barrier, the ground littered with corpses and sticky with blood.

Every person had to produce an identity card at each barrier. The owner of a card bearing the ethnic origin 'Tutsi' was killed on the spot, or else thrust to one side to be killed later at the mob's convenience. Even those with Hutu on their card, but who happened to have too long a nose, or fine features, or long fingers – causing them to resemble a Tutsi – suffered the same fate.

What chance did she have, a tall, slim, fine-featured elegant lady? There was nowhere to hide, nowhere to escape. Yet returning home would bring no protection. There was no time to stop and think. They just had to keep going. But they had not gone far when they were spotted. Perhaps they were fortunate to be spotted by a soldier with a gun – at least their death would be relatively quick and painless, unlike those slowly hacked to death at the barriers.

The soldier demanded identification. There was no point in trying to hide it – that led to death as well. Calmly, she passed him her card.

Tutsi. Death sentence.

Her four children squeezed close to her, looking up at the soldier with big, round, frightened eyes. He tossed away the card and raised his gun. As he did so, to her astonishment she heard the voice of her seven-year-old son.

'What are you killing us for, sir?' The youngster looked straight up at the soldier. 'We're only poor people, we don't have anything. Why do you want to kill us?'

She held her breath. For a brief moment that felt like an eternity, the soldier did not move. Then, to her absolute amazement, he lowered his gun.

'OK, kid. You can go then. Off you go, all of you.' The harshness in his face had gone. His eyes were full of sadness and confusion. They could hardly believe what was happening. He had spared their lives!

But where could they go? There were thousands more soldiers, ready to kill where this one had spared. It was an impossible situation. Then, with a poise and calm she had never before experienced, she asked the soldier to help. He hesitated for a moment, then motioned to them to get into a nearby vehicle.

'I'm taking these ones up to Remera. I'll kill them up there,' he called across to a group of soldiers standing not far off.

The children sat in terrified silence in the back of the car. Would he really help them, or was he merely prolonging the agony before disposing of them? They were entirely at his mercy. There was absolutely nothing they could do – except pray. For some reason, God had spared them the first time. Perhaps God would spare them again; they were in his hands.

At Remera, they found the killing was even more frenzied. They knew they would not last one minute if left there. 'Where do you live?' the soldier asked them.

She explained the way back to their house, and

without stopping he drove them to the door. They bundled out of the car and dived straight into the house. In their short absence it had been broken into, but not destroyed. They huddled together in an inner corridor in the dark, awaiting their fate. Surely someone has seen them return. It would not be long until they were found and taken to their death, along with those whose bodies lined the streets. They waited, and they prayed.

In the end, no one ever did come back for them. It seemed that their area had been cleared of Tutsis while they were away, and so no one thought to come looking again. They stayed there for weeks, surviving off what food they had had in the house, until the RPF took over Kigali.

'I believe my child was an angel sent by God,' she told us. 'Why else would that soldier have spared us? It's a miracle of God that we're alive today, no other reason.'

We all nodded in agreement, and there was silence in the car for a few moments.

There was nothing more to be said. How could I even *begin* to understand the agonies of what she had been through? Only those who have lived through such hell can enter into the nightmare of others. I can listen, weep with them over the tragedies, rejoice with them over their divine protection. But I can never really claim to understand.

Delicious smells like a Chinese restaurant met me as I opened the door back at the house, and Bob Marley blasted forth from the music centre. We were staying for a few days in a convenient spot in the centre of Kigali. It was the home of a British missionary family who were out of the country for a while, but their houseboy Deo was running the home very competently in their absence – and looking after us very well.

I called hello to Deo, but it was totally drowned out, so I followed the sounds of activity through to the kitchen. Clad in an apron, fingers covered in flour, he jumped as I came in.

'Oh, you gave me a fright. I didn't hear you coming in.' He grinned as he tossed a few pieces of marinated beef into the sizzling wok.

'I'm not surprised.' I shouted back. 'What a racket! Can I turn it down a bit?'

Deo was a bright young Rwandan and picked up new ideas quickly. He had learned a lot about cooking from the family for whom he worked, and was now in his element putting his lessons into practice. Tonight it was Chinese stir-fry beef. I had not eaten lunch, but even the mouth-watering smells did not tempt me. I had no appetite at all. I left him putting the finishing touches to the meal, singing along to Bob Marley, and went to lie down for a few minutes.

After supper I settled myself down at the table to write my diary. My head was still spinning. There was so much I wanted to express, and the best way seemed to be by writing it down. Deo sat in a corner chair, reading. But he was not concentrating; he was watching me.

'Why are you angry, Lesley?' He looked at me with his head slightly turned to the side.

I looked up from my writing. 'What makes you think I'm angry?' I had not realised how much my preoccupation with the day's events was visible in me.

'You're very quiet. I think you're not very happy.'

'I suppose you're right.' I thought for a moment. 'I'm

angry, sad, shocked, disbelieving – all rolled into one. To be honest, I don't really know how I feel.' We had talked a little about the day's events, so he knew the source of my distress.

Deo was thoughtful for a moment. 'I think it's impossible to forgive. The guys who wanted to kill me, the ones who looted my house, they're still around. If I go back to live at home, they still might kill me. I can't forgive them.'

I sat back in my chair and took a deep breath. I so much wanted just to concentrate on the day's events in my own life, but here before me was a young Christian with big issues he needed to discuss. After years of mocking Christianity, Deo had finally accepted it as the Truth, and just before the war he had committed his life to God. It was knowing and experiencing the reality of God in his own life that had kept him going through exceptionally tough circumstances in the early months. His new faith had been rigorously tested right from the beginning, and with that came profound questions.

Forgiveness. This was Deo's problem, but was it not mine too? Was he not right when he said I was angry? Angry towards those who had murdered my husband, my friends. Angry towards the soldier in our house. I had a heart full of anger, not forgiveness.

Yes, I could well understand Deo's question. How was *I* to forgive these people? Never in my life had I been on the receiving end of such injustice; never had I been so close to deliberate and intentional evil. Deo had been a Christian for only a few months, but I had been one for many years. Did I *really* believe what I read in the Bible? What help could I be to Deo if I did not accept it for myself? Anyway, what did the Bible really say about forgiveness?

'Where's your Kinyarwandan Bible?' I asked him. 'Bring it through.'

I fetched mine, and together we looked up some of the passages about forgiveness.

'Look at Matthew, chapter six, verses 14 and 15: "For if you forgive men when they sin against you, your heavenly Father will also forgive you. But if you do not forgive men their sins, your Father will not forgive your sins." Wow! That's pretty clear. And it's Jesus saying it. Here's another bit from Paul's letter to the Colossians, chapter 3, verse 13. Have you found it? "Forgive as the Lord forgave you."'

The verses cut right into my own heart. They were very clear; there were no exceptions noted. Forgiveness was a command, whether I liked it or not, and there were no conditions attached. Of course I wanted God to forgive me. Maybe the things I had done wrong seemed trivial in comparison with the murder and torture others had committed, but they were wrong none the less. Together, Deo and I wrestled with God's commands. Reading them in the Bible was one thing, but putting them into practice was a different matter.

'But how can I, after all they have done?' Deo insisted. Another passage came to mind.

'Deo, remember when Jesus was hanging on the cross? He'd been tortured, lied about, made a fool of, and then finally killed, but he was an innocent man. He hadn't done *anything* wrong in his life. Do you remember what he said? He said "Father, forgive them, because they don't know what they're doing." If anyone had reason to refuse to forgive, surely *he* had.

'And if Jesus could forgive after all that, surely we have to too. It's tough. Of course it's tough! Did anyone ever tell you being a Christian was easy?'

It was beginning to make sense to us both, but there was more to come. Deo's mind was full of questions. What about reconciliation? Who will go to heaven? So what does it really mean to be a Christian anyway?

We talked on till late in the evening, until we were both too tired to go on. It was not how I had planned to spend the evening, but God knew what I needed. I wrote in my diary that night, 'Do I really believe what I say, when faced with what I saw today? I realise that I do – passionately. It isn't just empty words that have no relevance in such an awful situation. I *know* it's true. The words of Jesus are *extremely* tough to obey when faced with such wickedness and injustice. But they are clear, and we have his example to follow, and his Holy Spirit to help us.'

By the time I went to bed, my mind was no longer in a spin and the heaviness in the pit of my stomach had begun to ease. What a relief not to have to carry the weight of bitterness and anger any more. I thanked God for the reality of forgiveness.

But I am slow to learn, and it was not the last time I would have to struggle with that question.

11

Discovering the Truth in Butare

Before Jennifer and I went our separate ways – she to return to the UK, and me to stay a further two weeks in Rwanda – there was one last place we wanted to visit together. This was Butare, the university town in south-west Rwanda to which Charles had fled soon after the war had begun.

Charles's sister Diane and his other sister's husband, Claude, had agreed that we should travel there together in their rickety old pick-up. It was a bit of a squash with Claude, Jennifer and I crammed into the front seat. I was practically sitting on the gear stick. The passenger window did not close properly, and the window behind us had a large crack across it.

Yet it was not nearly as draughty for us as it was for Diane in the open part of the pick-up. She had wrapped herself up well, a scarf on her head and two *kangas* around her legs and shoulders. To make the journey a little more comfortable for her, there was an old car seat wedged into the back.

This was the first time Claude and Diane had travelled any distance outside Kigali since the war had ended. But if they were unsure of the security situation on the roads, they did not show it.

Diane wanted as much as I did to visit the places where Charles had last been seen, and to speak to the people who were last with him. Perhaps, just perhaps, we might find some new information as to his whereabouts. I was still holding on to a tiny fragment of hope.

The road heading south-west was not very familiar to me; I had only been to Butare twice in my five years in Rwanda. However, that was twice more than Charles had. We had often talked of going there together, but we never did. I ached inwardly at the irony of the circumstances that had forced him to travel there for the first time, along this very road. What was going through his mind? Had he any idea of what lay ahead of him?

Charles was said to have been given a lift by someone in the army who was evacuating his own wife and children across to Zaire. Perhaps it was the same man who had been so helpful when Charles had sat his motorbike test. For those who were not prepared to pay a bribe, there was normally little chance of obtaining a licence – unless, that is, you had friends in the right places who could follow up a genuine application. Whoever it was, they were taking a big personal risk by transporting a Tutsi all the way to Butare through so many heavily manned road blocks.

The road twisted and wound along the crest of the hills giving superb views on both sides. There was mile upon mile of hills and valleys, green and luscious, covered from the peaks downwards with tiny homes and cultivated fields. There seemed to be more sign of activity in this area, and the land was better maintained than in the south-east.

For a brief moment I would marvel again at the

beauty of Rwanda – then suddenly there would be a little row of houses by the side of the road, with the middle one smashed to smithereens. Yet again, I would be jolted harshly back into reality.

We had left Kigali in brilliant sunshine, but by the time we reached Butare black clouds were beginning to roll across the sky. There would be some heavy rain before too long.

None of us was familiar with the town, so it took us a little while to find the Episcopal Church diocese. Eventually we spotted it: an impressive red-brick church stood by the roadside, and some 50 metres down the side of the hill were the various houses and buildings of the church compound.

The bishop's house was a solid-brick and cement building with a dark-green metal door and thick green metal bars on the windows. We had not informed anyone in advance of our visit, so we were not sure who we would find. For quite some time we stood waiting on the doorstep, until at last there was a response, the door was opened and we were invited inside. It was midday.

We explained who we were to a smiling, rather nervous lady, whom I took to be the bishop's wife. She welcomed us, inviting us to sit down; there was not much conversation.

I looked around at the little room where we were sitting. It was crammed full of solid furniture in good condition, and umpteen ornaments and crafts. The walls were adorned with photographs of the bishop on special occasions. Presumably, this house had not been touched. If only Charles had been invited to stay here instead of in the guest house down the hill . . .

I was beginning to think the bishop was not in, when

he finally appeared. We stood up to greet him, and once again explained who we were. It was the first time any of us had met him. For the first twenty minutes or so he told us in some detail of the terrible time he had had back in April, of how some of the windows in his house had been broken and the contents totally looted.

I was surprised to hear him say this, considering the house seemed to be so full of possessions. 'Well, I was able to get some furniture from the houses of our missionaries who had left,' he replied when I asked him about this. 'And what of the personal items, the photographs on the walls?' I asked. He explained: 'You see, people came to tell me that they had seen my photographs on sale in the local shops, so I was able to go and bring them back.'

The bishop was clearly rather pleased to have such a well-equipped house. Such an attitude seemed singularly inappropriate to me, considering the enormous loss of human life that had resulted from the genocide in this area – and in particular considering that we were here to investigate the disappearance of Charles, my husband, Diane's brother.

When he had finished telling us his own problems, he then began to explain the events leading up to Charles's arrest. He talked slowly and without emotion, pausing reluctantly from time to time to allow me to translate for Jennifer.

Arriving in Butare on Friday, 15 April, Charles had first gone to a friend's house. Perhaps he thought they might continue on together to Burundi, as this friend had worked on the border control. But his friend had already left, so Charles asked to stay at the diocese, declining the offer of a lift all the way to Zaire.

He checked in at the diocese guest house, and was given room no. 9. The following day, Saturday, he had gone into town to buy a few things at the market, and on Sunday he joined with the other local Christians for a service in the cathedral. During this time, Charles was regularly invited for meals by one of the other pastors on the compound. I was grateful that at least one person had obviously shown him some care and concern.

Even by mid-April, it was apparently still quiet in Butare. There were road blocks manned by soldiers, but they were for checking cars only, not pedestrians. However on the Tuesday, after the moderate prefect of the city had been removed and replaced by an extremist, the militia had begun to set up many more road blocks. They were stopping and checking everyone on the streets, killing people on the spot on the strength of their ID cards alone. Clearly, it was now impossible for Charles to leave even the diocesan compound.

I could not imagine the fear he must have experienced, being in a strange place where he knew almost no one and knowing his life was in the balance. Charles loved his country, and had always been positive and optimistic about its political future. How it must have broken his heart to be caught up in the extremist madness that had overtaken it.

The following day, the Wednesday, the bishop had called a meeting of all the pastors to discuss the situation. But we were not told the outcome of that meeting, nor were we given any indication as to how Charles was coping with the situation. The bishop was simply relating a series of events to me. We listened on without interrupting, except from time to time to ask him to pause while I translated for Jennifer. The bishop shifted restlessly in his comfy armchair, seeming somewhat annoyed at having his speech interrupted, and continued in English. So then I had to translate into Kinyarwanda for Diane!

'On Thursday four men in soldier's uniforms with guns came straight to his room, and knocked at the door,' he continued. 'He opened the door, and they ordered him to go with them.'

'Was anyone else with him?' I asked, surprised at the amount of detail the bishop knew.

'Oh no. He was alone. It wasn't until after he had gone that one of the other pastors came to see me and said "They've taken Bilinda."'

For a moment I remembered the report I had been given in August by a friend who had returned to Rwanda and spoken to the bishop. The end result was the same, but the details were significantly different. Originally the bishop had reported having a conversation with the soldiers, and that he watched them drive away with Charles in their car. Now he was telling us that he knew nothing until after it was too late. Something did not fit. These thoughts flitted through my mind and then drifted away. For the time being I was taken up completely with the starkness of what I was hearing.

So it was true. Charles had indeed been taken from this very place. It wasn't somebody else. He didn't escape at the last minute. He was captured.

The bishop finally finished his story. There was silence. My eyes stung and my stomach felt like lead. 'Thank you for explaining all that,' I managed at last. 'Do you think we could visit room no. 9 where he was?'

'Well, there's not much point really,' he replied. 'It's

all been redecorated. It's not the same now – it's being made into an orphanage.'

'I don't mind,' I replied softly. 'I would still like to see.'

I looked across to Jennifer and she nodded affirmatively.

'Very well then, if you want to,' the bishop replied.

He pulled himself to the edge of the chair, and leaning heavily on the padded arms, he propelled his body slowly forward and upward. We waited as he shuffled through to the back of the house. No one spoke.

A few moments later he reappeared with a key, and handed it to his son. 'Go and open up the guest house for them.'

A few yards down the hill from the bishop's house stood a long, narrow building. The outside was clean and fresh, having obviously been recently white-washed. We followed the boy up the half-dozen steps, and stepped inside as he held open the door. It was cool and there was a strong smell of paint. Our foot-steps echoed as we walked along the long narrow corridor.

I looked into each room as we passed: 6, 7, 8. They were almost empty, more like prison cells. Finally we reached room no. 9. I pushed open the door and stepped inside. Jennifer was right behind me, but the others had stayed outside. It was probably about 10 foot square, with a bare metal bed in the middle and a tatty rush mat rolled up on the floor.

'Would you like some time on your own?' Jennifer asked. 'I'll wait outside if you like.'

I nodded silently.

Closing the door gently behind her, I unrolled the

mat and knelt on the floor. In my handbag I had a photo of Charles – a happy, smiling, handsome Charles. I propped it up in front of me, but could contain myself no longer. My whole body groaned in agony and grief as the tears dropped steadily on to the mat. Charles, my dear Charles. So this is where you spent your last days, a lonely little room, among folk you didn't know. What were you feeling? What were you thinking? What agonies of heart and mind were you going through?

For most of my month in Rwanda I had found myself listening to, and sharing with, those whose loss was much greater than mine. Sometimes a sole survivor had watched his whole family brutally murdered before his very eyes. But here, in this small room, I felt the enormity of my own grief. I tried to pray, but there were no words to say. So I just opened my heart to Jesus, to allow him to deal with the sadness in it. And as I did so, I lifted my eyes upwards and began to feel the heaviness lift. It was as though Jesus was gently asking me, 'Why do you mourn in this empty room? Charles is not here any more. He's in heaven!'

That's true! I said to myself. His body may be lying somewhere in the forest, but he doesn't need it any more. He has a new body now. All of his suffering and torment are finished for ever.

It was even a comfort to think that he most probably had been shot, since it was soldiers who took him. Otherwise, had he been taken by the militia, it would have been a much more horrible death.

'Yes, Lord. Thank you,' I whispered through my tears. 'Thank you that this life is not all there is. Thank you that there is *much* better to come in heaven. And that Charles is there with you, even now.'

I wished I could have stayed there for longer. It was

almost as if Charles's presence was there with me. But I was conscious of the threatening black clouds overhead. Rain was imminent, and there was certainly not room for the four of us in the front of the pick-up. So reluctantly I stood up, walked back into the corridor, and joined Jennifer on the doorstep.

She put an arm around my shoulders. 'Would you like to go back in and pray for a bit?'

'It's OK, Jennie. I'll be all right.' But her compassion and care touched me, and I dissolved into tears again. So there on the grass in front of the guest house she held me firmly in her arms and prayed. There had been many times over the last few weeks when I had been grateful for Jennifer's company and support, but none so much as at that moment.

We rejoined Diane and walked slowly up the grassy path towards the bishop's house. Diane could see my distress. '*Wihangane*,' she said to me gently but quite firmly. 'Be patient.' It was the standard response to any trouble or sadness in this country. How often had I heard it before: 'Be patient!' It was not easy for Diane to see this display of emotion from me, but I had held back for long enough.

'I can't be patient at the moment. I'm sorry, but this is just the way we *Bazungu* are.'

She seemed to understand.

The bishop was waiting by his house when we returned; he said nothing.

'Was there anything of Charles's left behind in the room after he had gone?' I asked, presuming that he would have had to leave empty-handed.

'Well, yes, actually. He left his clerical robes. Would you like them?'

I hesitated. What would I do with his clerical robes? In the end, I decided to take them anyway. No doubt I would find someone who would appreciate having them.

The bishop disappeared into the house; we waited. The sky was growing more ominous by the second, and a cool wind was whipping up. There would be a downpour any minute.

Eventually he reappeared with a black robe and white surplice. I held up the surplice. It was crumpled and grubby, yellow sweat stains under the arms. Charles would have been disgusted by it, I thought. He was always so meticulous about his hygiene. I knew Charles's black robes well, having ironed them many a time before a Sunday morning service. These were not his – the material was much too lightweight. I handed them back.

'I don't recognise these at all. I don't think they're his.'

He returned back inside, and reappeared with a grey clerical shirt.

'I can't find the others at the moment. But is this maybe his?'

It looked a little familiar, so I took it.

Claude was keen to get away and there was clearly no point in staying any longer. There was nothing more to be said. Probably we would never know exactly what had happened over those last days of Charles's life.

During our time in Rwanda we had heard of remarkable acts of courage and self-sacrifice, but we had also heard of situations where victims could have been saved by colleagues, neighbours or even family members – but they were not. In the myriad of differing interpretations of an event, who could ever tell the truth, or the struggles of an individual's heart in the heat of a crisis? Only God knew.

I felt no anger or bitterness. Just sadness, numbed by all that we had seen and heard that day.

12

Picking Up the Pieces

Where could I hide? I wondered. Perhaps in the scrub and bushes at the side of the road? No, the militia would scythe them down like grass. What about down that deep drain? But if it rained I'd drown. Maybe in the toilet in the basement of the church? . . .

How many times had I walked around the streets of Kigali imagining the terror people must have felt as they tried to escape from the death squads. What would I have done if it had been me who was being hunted down? Would I have fled? Would I have hidden?

But I was not in Rwanda any more; I was in Kenya. I was standing in a queue in a large Nairobi bank, surrounded by very ordinary people doing very ordinary things. My month's visit was over; Rwanda was behind me now. I should have felt safe.

Yet the memories were still so acute – the sights, the stories, the smells and the sense of fear – that even as I thought of it I could feel my heart racing and I struggled to fight back the tears. How will I ever be able to begin to explain these horrors to the folks back in the UK? I thought. They were experiences too deep, too painful, too unbelievable to tell. Yet they are true; they really happened. Will anyone understand? Will anyone take the time to listen?

I had wanted to stay on in Rwanda. It was the only place on earth where people could understand what I was going through. It was where Charles's family was, where my memories of him were so real. To leave all of this behind would be to distance myself, to put a lid on that whole period of my life.

I was also looking forward to going home, though – to the safety, the predictability, the security of life in Britain. One month of living on a knife edge, going through an emotional mangle, was quite enough. I desperately wanted a break, to stop for a while and take stock of the situation.

The daily hustle and bustle of life in my sister Sue's home in Edinburgh brought me back down to earth with a gentle bump. It was good to have some routine and normality around me, and of course their supportive company. Yet I felt as though I were existing on two levels. Superficially I was fine and functioning normally, but all the time I was churning up inside, overwhelmed by the experiences of the past month that were acutely embedded in my memory. I could keep going – just as long as no one asked me anything about Rwanda and my recent visit there. On the rare occasions when I was able to find a response to people's concerned questions, and give just a tiny glimpse of what others had been through, I often found the questioner so overwhelmed that *I* ended up comforting *them*.

And yet I wanted to shout about it from the rooftops. I wanted to shake people out of their comfortable complacency and shock them with the reality of life in Rwanda. 'How would you feel if you were walking over your vegetable garden and discovered it was a mass grave?' I wanted to ask. 'Or if you learned that your dog had stayed alive for six months by eating dead human flesh left rotting over the hillsides? Or that your niece had died on your sister-in-law's back, clubbed to death by a heavy wooden stick spiked all around with nails?'

I wanted to tell of the amazing courage I had found among so many who had survived; those who had miraculously escaped death through God's protection; those who had risked (and some who had lost) their lives to protect others; those who had seen their families murdered before them, and yet were able to forgive the killers. Such people had an understanding of the preciousness of life, and a maturity in their Christian faith that left us in the West so far behind. I wanted to speak of them too.

I could not say anything, though, for fear of breaking down completely, so I always ended up with something bland like, 'It was shattering. I feel as though I've experienced every possible emotion that exists, and I'm still shellshocked by it all.' The result was a feeling of isolation and loneliness, cut off from those closest to me because of this large part of me that no one else could identify with. I struggled hard to know how to deal with it.

Jennifer had arranged a debriefing session for us both a couple of weeks after my return. It was to be with a pastor experienced in helping people through highly traumatic experiences in their lives. It sounded like a good idea, but as the meeting drew nearer I began to hesitate.

'I'd been looking forward to time with the debriefing chap,' I wrote one evening in my diary, 'but now I feel I don't really want to talk about it. What's the point? Either I survive by keeping my memories cold and clinical, shut away in the hidden recesses of my mind, which will surely harden me, or I enter into the horror and sadness of what I say, at huge emotional cost as I break down and weep. And that's exhausting.' In the end I did pour it all out – even the worst things that up until then I had not been able to speak of to anyone – and it was a great help.

'It's like these old ciné films,' Jennifer said as we sat chatting afterwards exhausted by the day's emotion. 'You know, the kind on two big reels. When one reel finishes it spins round and round until you connect up the end to the empty reel, and then it can gradually unwind.'

She was right. Up until now the reel had been spinning around wildly inside of me with no outlet, but now the process of connecting it to another reel had begun, and so giving the opportunity to offload gradually – thus restoring some sort of peace and consistency in my life.

In November we began to talk through the possibility of holding a memorial service for Charles. It was now as clear as it ever could be that he had been killed. There was no body and no grave, but I did not want that he should simply fade from our memories and be forgotten. It was important that we should acknowledge his death publicly and give thanks to God for the life he lived.

Yet it was going to be very difficult. Yes, we could thank God for his life, and we could thank him because we know Charles is in heaven. But he died a violent death, and no one could rejoice in that; and at such a service Charles would represent nearly one million other Rwandans who also died violent deaths. There was nothing to celebrate in that either.

We fixed the service for 3 December 1994, but as the date drew near my mind was a blank as to what I should say. Various friends and family were to be involved – in readings and tributes, in prayer and preaching, and in song. There was so much I could say, but my mind was still so overwhelmed and confused by the struggles of the past months that it seemed impossible to sift through it all.

A couple of days before the service I listened to a taped sermon I had found from a couple of years back, from my church in Enfield. It was entitled 'Authentic Christianity in a Hostile World – An Unusual Perspective'. It was so directly relevant that I felt it must have been given just for me! The message was about the great apostle Paul struggling with God over a 'thorn in his flesh', some kind of problem, illness or sadness that he repeatedly asked God to take away. Yet it was not removed.

Why? Why did God not answer his prayers? Why did God not answer *my* prayers? A sense of awe grew in me as I realised what the Lord was saying to me through this. Paul's 'thorn in the flesh', whatever it may have been, left him feeling weak and helpless, but God said to him, 'My grace is sufficient for you, for my power is made perfect in weakness' (2 Corinthians 12:9). Paul realised that he had come to the end of his *own* strength, but that he had *all* the strength he needed from Christ. 'For when I am weak,' he said, referring to his own resources, 'then I am strong' (2 Corinthians 12:10b) – strong, that is, in Christ's resources.

I certainly identified with Paul in his sense of weakness, but I also had the same resources available to me as he did – and as did Grace, Beatrice, Etienne, Emeralde and so many others – which is the strength of

Christ to sustain us. I realised afresh that through these periods of agony, the paradox of God's ways is that he actually brings strength out of weakness. That was part of the unusual perspective – so different from the way the world sees tragedy.

I had seen that time and time again in my Rwandan friends – their patience, strength, and yes, even joy, in the midst of the most tragic circumstances, and how these overflowed in their lives, bringing comfort and help to the broken lives around them. And so also in my circumstances, perhaps God would actually bring more blessings by *not* answering my prayers in the way I had thought was best. Perhaps, in his mysterious and paradoxical ways, he would touch many more people through Charles's death than if he had dramatically rescued him, as I had of course wanted.

Charles is now infinitely better off in heaven than he would have been living through that hell on earth; and as for those nearest to him who grieve, myself and his family, the Lord was clearly sustaining and comforting us.

No one could have wanted such pain, such sadness, such tragedy as has taken place in Rwanda, but these are the inevitable consequences of a fallen world, a world that has chosen to reject God and his ways. If my heart had been broken by all the sorrows, then how much more, I realised, must it grieve God's heart to see the people he had created, to whom he had given free will, use their freedom to turn their backs on him. Yet God was not sitting back, wringing his holy hands in despair. Did he not, through the resurrection of Jesus, transform the whole of history, bringing hope and new life out of seeming disaster?

My thinking was becoming clearer now. This was

not a defeat. It was not the end. In a strange kind of way, I felt as if it were the beginning of something new, as if in some small way God was bringing something positive out of Charles's death and, in the longer term, out of the whole tragedy that was and still is Rwanda's.

By 3 December my heart was once again at peace. The memorial service was a very special and significant occasion, respectful and sombre, yet confidently praising God for the reality of heaven and for his sovereignty in this present life.

Towards the end of the year a letter arrived from Grace in the Benaco refugee camp. It was the first letter since I had left her, and since starting her new job, so I was eager to find out how she was faring. In it she told me of how she had spent her first month's salary. I wondered what I would have done with my first salary if I was living in such desperate conditions as she was. Perhaps I would have bought some plastic sheeting to put over my grass hut to stop the rain from leaking in. Or maybe one or two pieces of clothing from the 'market' so I would not have to wear the same thing day in, day out. Or perhaps some decent food – some vegetables or fruit, tea or even meat – to supplement my meagre diet of dried corn and beans. Not Grace, though. She had never put her own needs first, and even now she had not changed. 'Of the money I earn, I give half of it to the poor people,' she wrote. I could hardly believe my eyes. Was she not one of those 'poor people' herself? I read on. 'Do you remember in Rwanda there were refugees wearing really worn-out clothes? There are many, many such people here too. I try to help the women who really have almost nothing to wear. For two ladies I bought small *kangas* ... And of the clothes you gave me, I gave one lady the blouse. God had given it to me for nothing, so if I receive anything I can help others who are very poor.' Here it was again. God using Grace to bring blessing and encouragement to those around her, in the midst of such a dreadful situation.

Every time I received a letter from Grace, or Etienne and Emeralde, or some other friend in the camps, I longed to be back there with them. And every time I received one from friends inside Rwanda, I longed to be with them too.

Yet I could clearly see that the time was not yet right to be heading back. There were other opportunities coming my way in which I had a definite role to play.

One of these, which was taking up an increasing amount of my time and energy, as well as that of my sister Sue and her husband Cameron, was the setting-up of a charitable trust in Charles's memory.

So many of Rwanda's educated people had been slaughtered during the genocide that it was going to be an extremely difficult task for the country to get back on its feet again. There was an urgent need to train others in place of those who'd died, but opportunities for higher education within Rwanda were now severely limited.

Our aim was to help the country by providing the opportunity for a small number of Rwandans to continue their education to a higher level. They would then return to their homeland and be significantly involved in its rebuilding and redevelopment by passing on their skills and expertise to others.

Thus the Charles Bilinda Memorial Trust was established at the end of 1994. Our initial goals were to help a young Christian couple of mixed ethnic origin who were at the time living as refugees in Nairobi. The husband had worked in a responsible position in the field of agriculture up until the events of April 1994, and was hoping to do further postgraduate study in the field of 'Extension in Rural Development' at Edinburgh University's School of Agriculture.

Passing on skills in the field of agriculture and rural development would be essential in this land where the density of the population was thought to have been one of the contributing factors of the war, and where over 90 per cent of the population were subsistence farmers.

His wife's concern was to gain counselling skills so that she could then work with the many thousands of traumatised women and children who had been widowed and orphaned by the war. Both had lost several members of their families, and had themselves escaped in miraculous circumstances.

News about the Charles Bilinda Memorial Trust spread throughout Scotland and far beyond, and donations began to pour in. We were overwhelmed by the rapid and generous response we received, not only in finance, but also in kind and in the offer of skills. So much so, in fact, that just six months after the Trust had begun, on Friday 26 May 1995, our first Rwandan couple and their twenty-month-old son arrived in Edinburgh. Not only had we received the finance to see them through twelve months in Britain and an MSc at university, but people's gifts had also fully furnished and equipped a house for them.

In some ways we felt as though we were on the outside, looking in at something quite remarkable taking place; and yet ours was the privilege to be intimately involved, part of another of God's mysterious paradoxes: bringing blessings out of tragedy.

The date 2 January 1995 would have been our second wedding anniversary. Charles's birthday in November had passed uneventfully, and Christmas and New Year had come and gone without the trauma I had expected. I was beginning to feel more normal for the first time in ages, but as our anniversary approached, the heaviness in the pit of my stomach returned.

One year, three months and nineteen days. That was all the time we had had together. Why did it turn out like this? Why, oh why? I picked up my pen and began to write:

> 15 months and 19 days.
> Then suddenly, all is gone,
>   wrenched apart,
>   torn away.
> 'Till death us do part' we said.
> Who was to know?
> Who could have imagined?
> Why did God bring us together
>   under such unusual circumstances
>   – only to be shattered,
>   separated,
>   after such a brief time.
> For ever – in this life.
> Why, God, why?
>
> But how can I complain,
>   how can I question
>   'why me?'
> How can my self-centredness last
>   for more than a few minutes

when I consider you, and
all you have gone through
   – for me?
God is no stranger to death,
   to pain, to suffering,
   to separation from a loved one.

Lord Jesus, you've been there already;
You didn't shy away,
You didn't drift up to heaven.
But you suffered
   the humility and degradation
   the injustice and disgrace
   the pain, the torment, the torture
   the agony of mind and body.
You've been there already
   and you know.

Your death wasn't wasted
But served a purpose
   – the greatest purpose of all,
That of securing our salvation.

So I believe
Charles's death cannot be wasted,
Because to those who love you
   all things work together for good.

How many times had I struggled with these questions, wrestling over them with God? Just exactly the same number of times as he had come back to me with his reassurance and comfort.

It was not that I had all the answers. Far from it. I was acutely conscious that there would be many questions I would put to God when I joined him in heaven. But I no longer needed to know all the answers; it was enough for me to know that God was in control and that he was bringing the best out of the worst.

For a long time during the spring of 1994 I thought I would never smile again. I could barely cope with one day's sadness at a time, and didn't give the slightest thought as to what the future might hold. Gradually, though, the way ahead began to open up, like the mist rising from the lake, slowly revealing the countryside around.

In early 1995 the opportunity came to make a thirty-minute documentary about my story for BBC Scotland. It was called *Moment of Truth*. Also, various people had suggested that I should record the experiences and testimonies of myself and others in a book. With these projects under way it now seemed right to part company with Tear Fund. Their understanding and support of me and my family over these traumatic months, and before, had been exceptional. It was going to be very hard to make the break.

I phoned up Pete Chirnside, the Scottish Co-ordinator for Tear Fund, to pass on the news. Over the past months Pete and I had travelled widely around Scotland, which gave me the opportunity of meeting up with the many Tear Fund Support Groups who had prayed for Rwanda, and specifically for Charles and myself. I was going to miss these opportunities, and the times with Pete and his family.

'But Lesley,' Pete insisted, in response to my news, 'that won't make any difference to us here. I've already booked you in for several speaking engagements. You're still very much part of the family.'

It was good to have these and other opportunities to speak publicly. People in the West need to hear of the shining examples of the lives of some of the Rwandan Christians.

Rwanda has seen so much horror and destruction. Perhaps some, who had not known it before the genocide, would write it off as a very dark and hopeless land. So often we have been presented, through our news media, with the most gloomy and negative aspects. But is that the whole story? Surely not.

In my mind's eye I can picture this darkness, but in its midst are hundreds of tiny lights, perhaps candles, dotted throughout the land and in the camps around. Wherever they are, these lights are shining brightly, pushing back the darkness, and revealing beauty and colour in their glow.

These lights are people. They are Grace and Beatrice, Etienne and Emeralde, Diane, Joelle and many, many others. They are those who have not compromised with the darkness around them, who have sought to bring light into the lives of others. They are those who gave their lives to protect others, and those who still risk them even today, because their love for Jesus and their fellow Rwandans is greater than their love for themselves.

Yet it is very hard for them. It is not easy being a candle in the darkness. Jesus came as a 'Light [shining] in the darkness, but the darkness has not understood it' (John 1:5). The pressure and problems around them are enormous, but for those who shine faithfully, the time will come when there will be no more darkness, no more pain or suffering.

It is my longing that the courage and humility of these Rwandan Christian 'lights', their joy and their deep faith, should shake us out of our comfortable complacency, and challenge us to real commitment to the Lord Jesus Christ, for whatever the future may hold.

Do everything without complaining or arguing, so that you may become blameless and pure, children of God without fault in a crooked and depraved generation, *in which you shine like stars in the universe* as you hold out the word of life (Philippians 2:14–16, my italics).

The Charles Bilinda Memorial Trust

Working for the future of Rwanda by providing Educational Opportunities and Support for Rwandans

☐ Please send me further information about the CBMT.

☐ I enclose my donation of £_____

☐ I enclose my Gift Aid donation (£250 or more)
£_____

If you are a tax payer the Trust can reclaim a further 33%.
A form will be sent to you.

☐ Please charge my Visa/Access/CAF Charity Card*
account no.

Name as on card _____

Expiry Date _____ Signature _____

☐ I wish to covenant _____ monthly/annually*
Please send me further details.

Name _____

Address _____

_____

_____

Please send to

The Charles Bilinda Memorial Trust
3 Millerfield Place
Edinburgh EH3 1LW

Tel/fax: 0131 667 1568

Scottish Charity No. SC 023113

* Delete as appropriate

Tear Fund

*An international Christian agency
working with churches in development
and relief throughout the world*

I would like to receive

☐ Tear Fund's quarterly magazine *Tear Times*

☐ Information on how to pray more effectively for the
work of Tear Fund throughout the world.

☐ Information on how to give effectively to the work of
Tear Fund throughout the world.

Name _____

Address _____

_____

_____

Please return to

Tear Fund
100 Church Road
Teddington
Middlesex TW11 8QE

Tel: 0181 977 9144
Fax: 0181 943 3594

Registered Charity No. 265464